SACRED LAND SACRED VIEW

UTAH
Colorado River
Dzil Ditl'ooii
(Blue Mountain)
Bears Ears Buttes
Blanding
VALLEY
OF THE
GODS
San Juan River
COMB RIDGE
Dzil Naajini
(Sleeping
Ute Mountain)
San Juan River
FOUR
CORNERS
Rainbow Bridge
Rabbit Ears
Naatsis'aan
(Navajo Mountain)
MONUMENT
VALLEY
CARRIZO MTNS.
Colorado River
Shiprock
Beautiful
Mountain
BLACK MESA
CHUSKA MOUNTAINS
1 Navajo Twins
2 Ch'ahlizhin
(Mexican Hat Rock)
3 Alhambra Rock
Goose Necks
of the San Juan
4 Mitten Buttes
5 Gray Whiskers Butte
6 Agathla Peak
(El Capitan)
7 Owl Rock
8 Chaistla Butte
9 Kayenta
10 Betatakin Ruins
11 Tsegi
12 Antelope House
13 White House
CANYON
DE
CHELLY
Tuba City
Little Colorado River
Chuska Peak
(Tohatchi
Mountain)
Gallup
ARIZONA
Dook'o'oosliid
WEST MOUNTAIN
(SAN FRANCISCO PEAKS)
NAVAJO SACRED

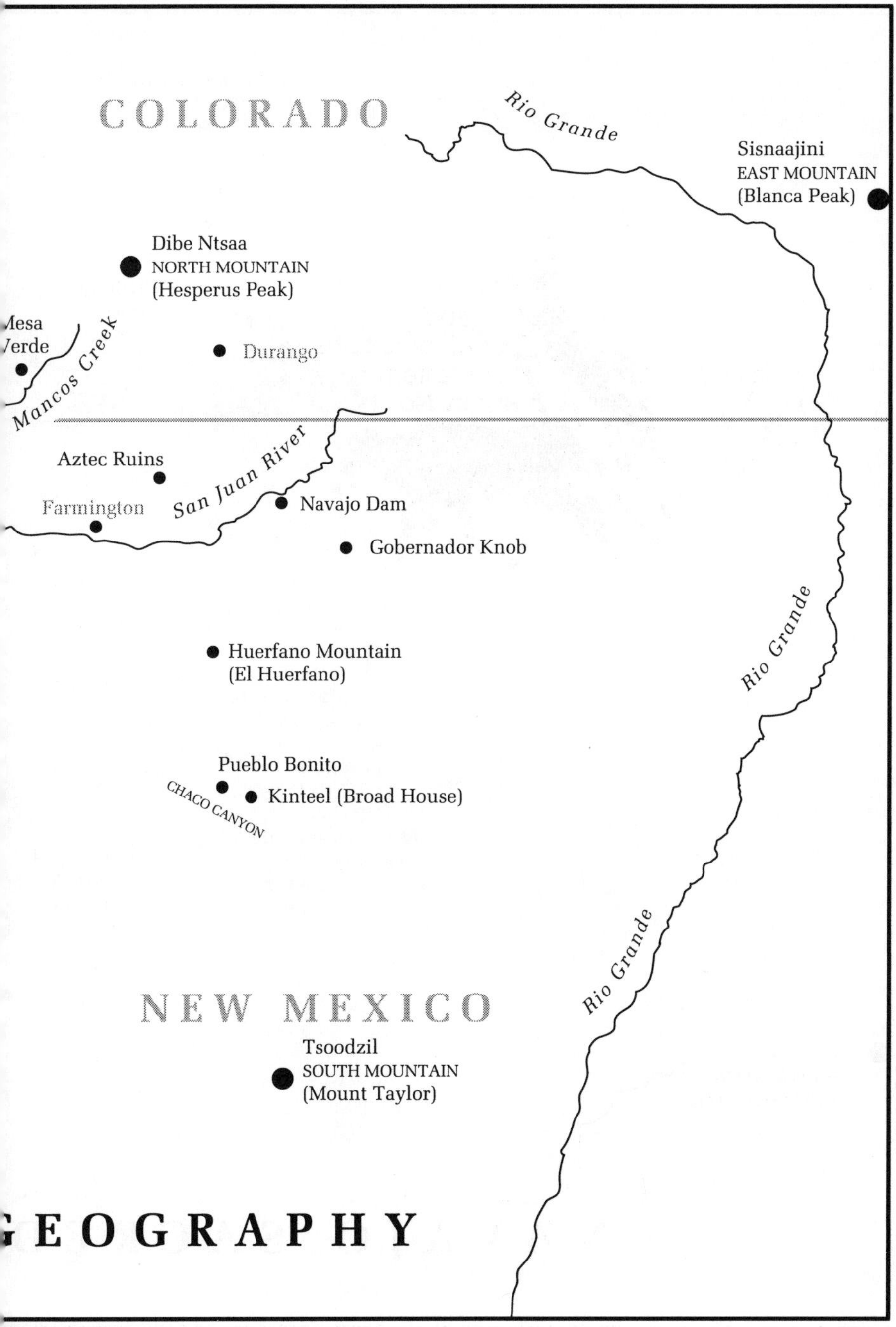
COLORADO
Rio Grande
Sisnaajini
EAST MOUNTAIN
(Blanca Peak)
Dibe Ntsaa
NORTH MOUNTAIN
(Hesperus Peak)
Mesa
Verde
Mancos Creek
Durango
Aztec Ruins
San Juan River
Farmington
Navajo Dam
Gobernador Knob
Rio Grande
Huerfano Mountain
(El Huerfano)
Pueblo Bonito
Kinteel (Broad House)
CHACO CANYON
Rio Grande
NEW MEXICO
Tsoodzil
SOUTH MOUNTAIN
(Mount Taylor)
GEOGRAPHY

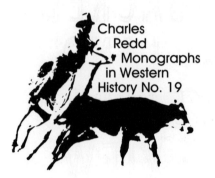

Charles
Redd
Monographs
in Western
History No. 19

SACRED LAND SACRED VIEW

Navajo Perceptions of the Four Corners Region

ROBERT S. McPHERSON

Brigham Young University
Charles Redd Center for Western Studies

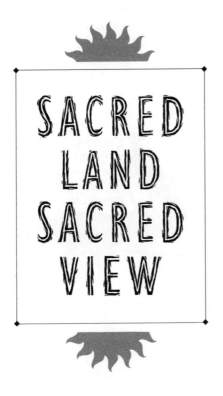

The Charles Redd Monographs in Western History are made possible by a grant from Charles Redd. This grant served as the basis for the establishment of the Charles Redd Center for Western Studies at Brigham Young University.

Center editor: Howard A. Christy

Cover: Merrick Butte, located in the Navajo Tribal Park, Monument Valley. To the Navajo, this and other similar rock formations are said to be water barrels and hold rain-producing qualities that can be appealed to through prayer. *(Photo by author)*

Library of Congress Cataloging-in-Publication Data

McPherson, Robert S., 1947–
Sacred land, sacred view : Navajo perceptions of the Four Corners Region / Robert S. McPherson.
p. cm.—(Charles Redd monographs in western history : no. 19)
Includes bibliographical references.
ISBN 1–56085–008–6
1. Navajo Indians—Religion and mythology. 2. Sacred space—Utah. 3. Pueblo Indians—Antiquities—Religious aspects. 4. Geographical perception. I. Title. II. Series.
E99.N3M516 1991
299′.782—dc20 91–33322
CIP

Third printing, 1995.
Printed in the United States of America.

Distributed by Signature Books, 350 S. 400 E., Suite G4, Salt Lake City, Utah 84111

Contents

Introduction

In 1978 I taught a developmental English class to Navajo college students in Montezuma Creek, Utah. When I handed out the midterm exam, the students, like students everywhere, clamored for extra credit, and so I related a brainteaser that I had learned recently. The story frame of the question stated that a man built a square house in which all sides faced the south. A bear walked by the house; what was the color of the bear? The expected answer was that, if all four sides of the structure faced south, the house would have to be built at the North Pole and that the bear would therefore have to be white. One student, however, arrived at a far different response. His reasoning took me to the four cardinal directions with their associated ceremonial colors and a short treatise on the power of bears. Although his answer was not the one expected, it was just as rational and more intellectual than the "correct" one. He received full credit and a thank you for teaching the teacher an important principle of culture and world view.

And so it is with this book—a book about a different perception. In an increasingly mechanistic, complex life, it is helpful to pause and look at the world through another pair of eyes. The Navajo world view provides such a glimpse, presenting a world where the commonplace becomes uncommon, the mundane holy.

On May 28, 1868, William Tecumseh Sherman met with the seven main chiefs of the Navajo nation held captive at Bosque Redondo. Four disastrous years of incarceration on an inadequate, sterile reserve had decimated the *Diné* (the People) physically and spiritually to the point that, to them, the only meaningful answer for life was to return to the high desert plateaus they had left. Barboncito, a well-respected leader, told Sherman:

> When the Navajos were first created, four mountains and four rivers were appointed for us, inside of which we should live, that was to be our country,

> and was given us by the first woman [Changing Woman] of the Navajo tribe. It was told to us by our forefathers, that we were never to move east of the Rio Grande or west of the San Juan rivers and I think that our coming here has been the cause of so much death among us and our animals. . . . Because we were brought here, we have done all that we could possibly do, but found it to be labor in vain, and have therefore quit it; for that reason we have not planted or tried to do anything this year. It is true we put seed in the ground but it would not grow two feet high, the reason I cannot tell, only I think that this ground was never intended for us. . . . I thought at one time the whole world was the same as my own country but I got fooled in it. Outside my own country we cannot raise a crop, but in it we can raise a crop almost anywhere; our families and stock there increase, here they decrease; we know this land does not like us, neither does the water. . . . It seems that whatever we do here causes death. Some work at the acequias, take sick and die; others die with the hoe in their hands; they go to the river to their waists and suddenly disappear; others have been struck and torn to pieces by lightning. A rattlesnake bite here kills us; in our country a rattlesnake before he bites gives warning which enables us to keep out of its way and if bitten, we readily find a cure—here we can find no cure. . . . I am speaking for the whole tribe, for their animals from the horse to the dog, also the unborn. All that you have heard now is the truth and is the opinion of the whole tribe. It appears to me that the General commands the whole thing as a god; I hope, therefore, he will do all he can for the Indians; this hope goes in at my feet and out at my mouth. I am speaking to you (General Sherman) now as if I was speaking to a spirit and I wish you to tell me when you are going to take us to our own country.[1]

Barboncito spoke in metaphorical language rooted in his reality. The land anchored him to a cosmic identity, a way of relating to the supernatural. Geography represented his culture's conscious and subconscious symbols of what was important and unimportant, what supported life and fostered death, how one should act and what to avoid. The importance of these deep-seated, intangible roots of belonging are recognized today as being just as important as the tangible, material things that sustain the body. Thus, Barboncito responded to what his culture determined to be important and practical, in opposition to what the military planners felt expedient.

This same type of misunderstanding persists today. Take, for example, the relocation of Navajos in the Big Mountain region of Arizona. The Hopi-Navajo Joint-use Area is a hotly contested territory in which the government is trying to remove Navajos from land now given to the Hopi tribe. The anguished cries and hostilities that have arisen from relocating older people have created a tension that seems unresolvable. While the white administrators of the relocation program have provided modern houses with running water, electricity, and a small yard space, many of the older people reject them for their traditional homes and a familiar, local setting. To borrow the title from Richard White's work, the Diné have planted in the soil their "roots of dependency" that lie curled around and imbedded within a local and regional mythological dependence upon the land. Shrines for prayers, places for plant gathering, land formations steeped in mythology, and a way of thinking cannot be easily exchanged for physical conveniences.

Just as desert plants depend upon their deep taproots to seek cool subsurface waters, leathery leaves to conserve moisture in the blazing sun, and a tough bark to protect against the elements, so too do the Diné shield themselves against the turmoil of daily life and discordant, modernizing influences. The land and its associated beliefs water and fertilize the mind, helping the Diné maintain their identity in the "center" of the universe. Typically, only half of a desert plant is visible, the rest remaining below the surface to nurture and stabilize. The Diné, who survive in a very physical, practical world, are also rooted and nurtured spiritually in the intangible teachings and philosophy of their culture.

The ancient Anasazi serve as a good example of what happens when those roots become weakened and too much emphasis is placed on the physical or visible part of existence. The Anasazi culture shriveled and died because the people transgressed the laws of the holy beings and of nature as they sought ease through power which they abused. Their example and the visible remains left behind serve as a reminder of death and destruction in the midst of life; of a holy way gone bad; of the duality of good and evil, the sacred and the profane, and correct values in opposition to misdirected practices. The Anasazi's failure sends a strong message to the Diné that nothing can survive unless it is vested with power which comes from the holy beings within each physical form.

Geography establishes one facet of this system of survival, a moral code with both positive and negative examples. Battle sites of the hero twins, the San Juan River, Comb Ridge, and Navajo Mountain are just a few of the positive examples that create boundaries and repeat the favorable pattern of protection and well-being throughout the Four Corners region. Negative examples of vice, competition, and destruction lie in the ruins, artifacts, and stories concerning the Anasazi; in rock formations associated with Coyote and his mischievous, disrespectful ways; in the places of witchcraft; and in locations where misbehavior has been punished.

Good cannot exist without evil, nor white without black. It is important that the Diné recognize both, not only from the practical standpoint of explaining why problems occur and evil exists, but also because understanding the relationship between the two enables an individual to control wrong. Gladys Reichard suggested that the best way to exorcise evil is to narrow its territory, restrict its possibilities, and then create a boundary over which it cannot pass.[2] In Navajo religion this boundary may be symbolized in the sand paintings of a ceremony, the flint arrowheads of the Twins, the fire poker that represents domesticity, the pungent odors of desert plants offensive to evil, or any number of other devices that speak of protection.

The land also addresses this issue from birth to death. Just as a mother may bury her newborn child's umbilical cord under a piñon tree near the home, signifying an attachment to the land, so too does every waking hour renew this bond through prayers, stories, and respectful behavior. As long as one shows proper reverence, the boundary of protection remains intact and life is harmonious. Defile the sacred or take lightly the holy beings and there is no safety.

While these beliefs hold true for many of the older people, what about members of the younger generation who have not been raised in the same tradition? This is a difficult question to answer and a more difficult one to quantify. I have the impression that within a generation or two only a few select people will live by the teachings discussed in this book. Although there are efforts to maintain traditional beliefs—such as those made by the Rough Rock Demonstration School, Navajo Community College, and various tribal curriculum programs—many teachings do not find their way into an integrated system of values that can override the loud voice of technology and twentieth-century culture. This is in no way to suggest that Navajo culture is doomed, that the younger people will face failure and poverty, or that everyone belongs to a lost generation. There will always be a Navajo people, and for some time yet they will maintain distinct cultural practices; the direction and rate of change is the issue. As they achieve their social, economic, and political goals, many of the older values will be discarded for a different understanding of what empowers the world and what is important.

According to Joseph Campbell, in order for a system of beliefs to be a viable force within a person's life, it must meet four criteria.[3] First, the belief must have a mystical function in which a person lives with awe and gratitude toward the supernatural forces of the universe. Second, it must be in tune with the knowledge and science of the times, giving an adequate explanation of how things occur that does not conflict with the understanding of the physical world. Third, it must "validate" the teachings and practices of what is morally acceptable in a certain culture. Last, it should be a guide to spiritual harmony and strength in a useful life.

For the older people raised with traditional Navajo values, these functions of mythology still provide a vital explanation of how the world was created and empowered with supernatural forces. For the younger generation, these teachings are not as available as the white man's schools that provide a nonreligious, secular explanation of the world and its forces. The result is both individual and community confusion. Some people follow the teachings of their parents, some the beliefs of the dominant culture, and others something in between.

There were two possible ways to write this book. One was to write solely to the scholarly community in the tradition of Gladys Reichard, Clyde Kluckhohn, Gary Witherspoon, John Farella, and others, to discuss the hermeneutics and exegesis of Navajo beliefs and thought. While the work of these scholars is invaluable, it often does not trickle down to the general audience and has little impact upon those living on or near Navajo land. At worst, this understanding becomes bottled up, serving only as mental gymnastics for a select few. Donald Worster, a leading writer in historical ecology, summarized the problem recently when he said, "If we get too obsessed with particularities, the public may not be truly helped by our writings to think clearly and coherently about the larger issues of our time—the relation of nature to capitalism, the collective myths and institutions of nations and civilizations, the workings of imperialism, the fate of the earth."[4]

I have chosen, instead, an approach that I hope will be useful to both the general public and the scholarly community, but most importantly to the Navajo people of the Four Corners region. This is their story, shared willingly with the understanding that the teachings and beliefs written herein will be given back to the younger generation. Elderly Navajos realize that, as rapid change bombards the youth, many of the beliefs accepted as part of Navajo culture will be lost if not recorded. Their desire to pass on this heritage was an important impetus to writing this book. The many hours spent in collecting, translating, transcribing, and writing will be well used if this goal is achieved.

Asdzaan Nez. "We were taught by our parents that Mother Earth is sacred, that it is a place where 'life is lived and buried,' and so it is forbidden to fight or in other ways bother our mother. That is why I leave it alone." Mary Jay, medicine woman, Aneth. *(Photo courtesy Harold B. Lee Library)*

Much of the material gathered is tied to Navajo myths and legends. Many of these are lengthy treatises that deal only in part with the topic at hand—that is, the importance of mountains, streams, clouds, ruins, and the like. Instead of recounting the entire story, some of which is already in print, I have grouped materials topically in order to emphasize their collective importance. Although this may somewhat violate the context in which an idea is given, it provides a clearer, fuller understanding of the depth of respect the Diné have for the land.

These thoughts shared by the Navajo people are as real as anything in the materialistic world of twentieth-century America, but it has not been until recently that myths and cultural beliefs have taken their rightful place in explaining the human experience. Men like Joseph Campbell, Victor Turner, Mircea Eliade, and Claude Lévi-Strauss have been in the forefront in defining these powerhouses of cultural values—values that were earlier considered merely quaint folk beliefs. Myths are increasingly being viewed as a holistic expression of what is important, acceptable, and desirable in a society. And we are becoming increasingly aware that myths determine *most* beliefs, regardless of a particular culture.

Take, for instance, something concrete—say, a mountain. Although a mountain is to many only an inanimate mass of earth and rock existing in a physical realm, Navajo myths teach of its mystical creation, its spiritual powers, and its purpose in relation to the people. In the white man's world, water, lumber, building plots, ski resorts, and mineral rights are the only attributes of the mountain. For the Diné, although some of these concerns are important, they are subordinate to the idea that man works through nature in establishing relationships. The ultimate expression of what is important to the Diné is found, not in things or empirical truth, but in relationships—to the earth, to spiritual forces, to other people. The myths, ceremonies, and prayers all speak to this concern and shape reality.

Today's society tries to corner the slippery eel of truth by pinning it down. People argue their points of view as if they know what truth is and feel that it is their duty to reveal it to those not as enlightened. While the Diné may have their own set of arguments, rarely will they dispute religion and beliefs. One day I took an hour-long cassette recording to Monument Valley to play to a group of medicine men and older people to see if a certain body of material was accurate. After playing part of the cassette, I asked the group for their response. One medicine man, serving as spokesman, indicated that it seemed good, but that I should not be concerned with what the gathering said. He went on, "That is how you were taught; then that is correct." There was no ultimate, specific truth or way of understanding, but rather room for thought and meditation. His view came partly from the varying teachings that serve as the basis for different Navajo ceremonies, and partly because of the way he personally perceived truth.

In a broad sense, truth, or lack of it, to the Diné may take three forms. There are truth, lies, and truth that exists but has not been seen. The first two categories are fairly straightforward; the last one belongs to the realm of myths and religion.[5] One does not have to see a supernatural being or event to know that it exists now or occurred in the past. Navajo beliefs, therefore, do not try to eliminate possibilities but rather incorporate them into an already existing framework. What is or is not accepted is based in the realities expressed in the myths, not just what is tangibly proven today. The roots of perception — what is practical, believable, and acceptable — are rooted in this religious, mythological view.

Mircea Eliade has observed that man wants to avoid being "overwhelmed by the meaninglessness of profane existence."[6] Through myths, prototypes of suffering and joy, pain and pleasure, good and evil are given in an explanation that contributes meaning to the vagaries of life. Both the good and the bad can be controlled because they are understood. When a taboo is broken or a god angered, an explanation of what went wrong is provided and a propitiation given. It is the myths that outline the cause-and-effect relationships by which this framework is understood.

Symbols of this mythology help condense into a few elements the meaning or essence of a cluster of thoughts. Referred to in anthropological literature as "polysemous and multivocal," symbols provide an impetus to react in certain ways. Joseph Campbell called them "affect images," images which speak to feelings that evoke a response.[7] Shared by groups of individuals and the culture as a whole, myths and their accompanying symbols are the lifeblood that courses through them and fosters the unique way of viewing the world in which they are rooted.

In the following pages, two seemingly independent topics — sacred geography and the Anasazi — are used to give a unique understanding not apparent to much of the white world.

To the Diné, everything has a spirit, is animate and rational, and holds a power that can be either helpful or destructive. The basis for this understanding is derived from stories — myths, legends, and tales — that teach the core perceptions of life. While thinking in the white world is often segmented into various branches of learning such as psychology, religion, history, and science, Navajo stories and beliefs combine such ideas in a holistic expression of the universe. Thus, the criteria of biology or physics should not be applied empirically in a one-on-one relationship to Navajo thought. Comparing the proverbial apples with oranges does not work. These two systems of thinking provide different ways of looking at the same thing which at times may be incompatible, at others mutually supportive. What does consistently occur, however, is a fuller appreciation of two cultures' views.

The land and its forces, the Anasazi and their ruins, serve as just such symbols to the Diné. In the following pages, dozens of examples illustrate this phenomenon, as the Diné interpret their environment through their beliefs. It is one of the central focuses of traditional values; it is a sacred land, a sacred view.

"North Mountain." One of four paintings by Harrison Begay depicting the personalities and qualities associated with each of the Four Sacred Mountains. North Mountain, or Dibé Ntsaa, is fastened to the earth by a rainbow, impregnated with jet, and covered by darkness. It has certain animals, plants, and holy beings dwelling either on or in this sacred form.
(Photo of painting courtesy Museum of Northern Arizona)

PART ONE

Power, Prayers, and Protection: Navajo Sacred Geography of the Four Corners Region

The Four Corners region is studded with dramatic geographical features. Towering mountains, sparse deserts, red rock cliffs, and lone sandstone spires call forth the imagination and awe of man's soul. Everett Ruess, a vagabond philosopher, captured the spirit of man's relation to the land as he traveled in the Kayenta–Monument Valley area of the Four Corners country. He wrote:

> Music has been in my heart all the time, and poetry in my thoughts. Alone on the open desert, I have made up songs of wild, poignant rejoicing and transcendent melancholy. The world has seemed more beautiful to me than ever before. I have loved the red rocks, the twisted trees, the red sand blowing in the wind, the slow, sunny clouds crossing the sky, the shafts of moonlight on my bed at night. I have seemed to be at one with the world. I have rejoiced to set out, to be going somewhere, and I have felt still sublimity, looking deep into the coals of my campfires, and seeing far beyond them. I have been happy in my work, and I have exulted in my play. I have really lived.[1]

Ruess's vision of the land was based on a personal ecstasy as the poet revealed his soul. But for the Diné, who lived here long before the white man ever saw this region, the land holds even deeper values that go to the core of Navajo ceremonial beliefs and perception. The earth is not just a series of dramatically poised topographic features that incite the wonder of man or beckon for exploitation, but is rather a living, breathing entity in an animate universe. The land with its water, plants, and animals is a spiritual creation put into motion by the gods in their wisdom. These elements are here to help, teach, and protect through an integrated system of beliefs that spell out man's relationship to man, nature, and the supernatural. To ignore these teachings is to ignore the purpose of life, the meaning of existence.

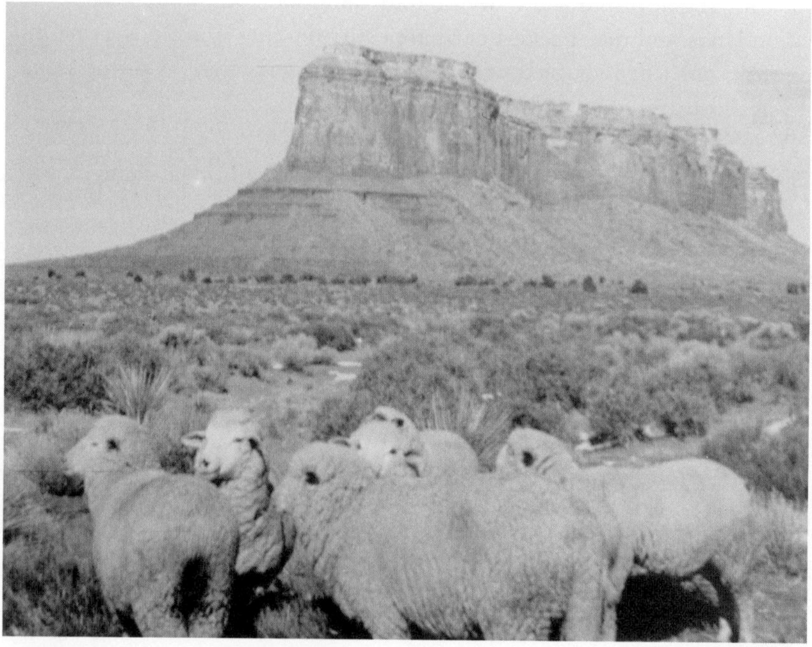

Eagle Mesa, on the northern edge of Monument Valley. "We treat our land with respect and want to continue to do so throughout generations to come. We will not forget, but we also want our children to remember." Buck Navajo, medicine man, Navajo Mountain. *(Photo by author)*

A number of general studies have attempted to explain Navajo views of the land.[2] While these studies describe many Navajo beliefs, they all fail to point to the integrated pattern those beliefs present. Each one dwells at length on the importance of the four sacred mountains—and rightly so—but then fails to move beyond to a single, in-depth geographical location to see conceptual patterns multiplied over a local landscape. To study the approximately twenty-four thousand square miles of reservation lands and the checkerboard area surrounding it is an overwhelming task; but when coupled with the varying interpretations of the same physical features, the work staggers into impossibility.

The purpose of this study is to look at one part of this Navajo universe—the Four Corners region—and show how traditional thought and values reflect a close observation of and appreciation for the land. Only by taking a comprehensive look at a small part of the reservation area can the intricacies of Navajo perception be applied to the mountains, earth, sky, rocks, rivers, plants, and animals to explain the symbiotic relationship between the Diné and their surroundings. What results is a rewarding view of life.

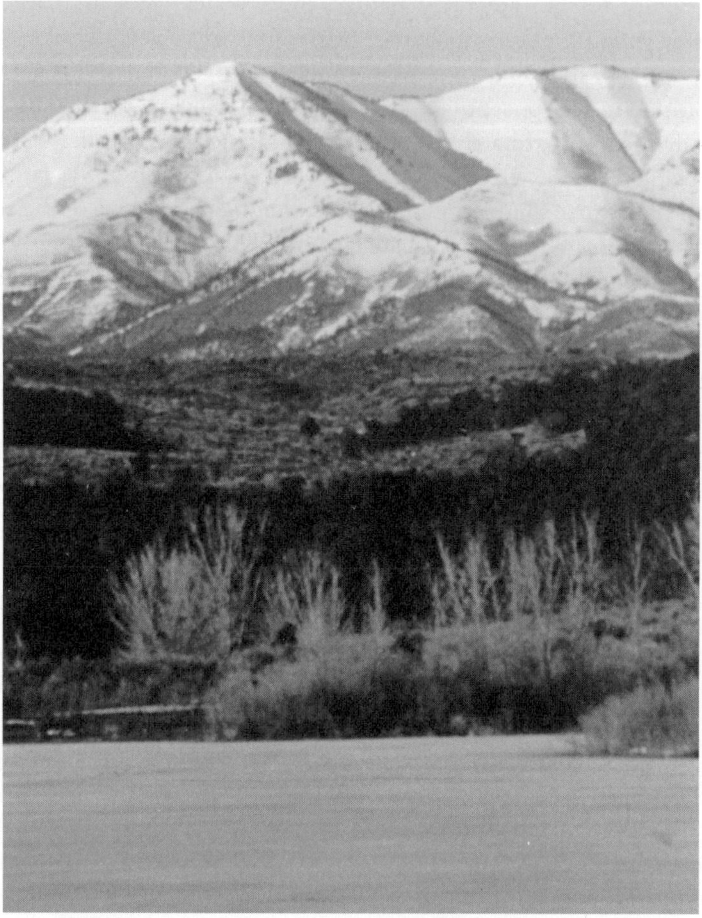

Blue Mountain, though not one of the four or six most sacred mountains, is still considered holy and powerful. During the time of creation, Jóhonaa'éí changed the location of this and other mountains to test the knowledge of his two sons, Monster Slayer and Born for Water.
(Photo courtesy Stan Byrd)

CHAPTER ONE

Mountains

The heart and soul of Navajo beliefs starts with the four sacred mountains. As the Diné emerged from the four worlds below this one, they entered into a place devoid of form. First Man had brought soil from the mountains in the fourth world, and so he fashioned from it four replicas of those left below, mixed sacred matter in each, planted them in the cardinal directions, and breathed into them to make them live and grow large.

In the east he put Sisnaajinii, or Blanca Peak, Colorado, placed in it white shell, covered it with daylight and dawn, fastened it to the ground with lightning, and assigned it the symbolic color of white. To the south went Tsoodził, Mount Taylor, in which he placed turquoise; he then covered it with blue sky, fastened it with a great stone knife, and gave it the color blue as its symbol. Dook'o'oosłííd, or the San Francisco Peaks, is the mountain of the west. Securing it to the ground with a sunbeam, First Man put abalone inside and covered it with yellow clouds and evening twilight, yellow being its color. Black is the color of Dibé Ntsaa, or Hesperus Peak in Colorado, the mountain of the north. It is fastened by a rainbow, impregnated with jet, and covered with darkness.

First Man formed two other mountains—Gobernador Knob and Huerfano Mountain—both of which are of deep religious significance but not comparable to the first four, from which pour the health and strength of the Navajo people. They each have a number of ceremonial names derived from mythology—titles such as Sun Mountain, Rain Mountain, Mist Mountain, Faultless Mountain, One with a Mind, Speaking Wisdom Mountain, Soft Goods Mountain, Hard Goods Mountain, Corn Mountain, Corn Beetle Mountain, Happiness Mountain, and Immortality Mountain.[1] All six mountains are called chieftains, and in each gods reside.

During this creative period Talking God and Calling God assumed guardianship of the mountains, dressing them in jewels, giving each two songs, and placing supernaturals within to gather the clouds and answer prayers. To the east live Talking God, Rock Crystal Boy, and Rock Crystal Girl; in the south are Black God, Turquoise Boy, and Turquoise Girl; the west are White Corn Boy, Yellow Corn Girl, and Abalone Girl; and in the north live Monster Slayer, Pollen Boy, and Grasshopper Girl.[2] They are there to help heal the sick, supply rain for crops, and provide protection from harm. Indeed, their role is all-encompassing in Navajo life. A medicine man, George Blueeyes, explains:

> These mountains and the land between them are the only things that keep us strong. From them, and because of them, we prosper. . . . We carry soil from the sacred mountains in a prayer bundle that we call dah ńidiilyéeh. Because of this bundle, we gain possessions and things of value, turquoise, necklaces, and bracelets. With this we speak, with this we pray. This is where the prayers begin.[3]

Each mountain has an inner form or holy being known as bii'istíín, or Those That Stand within Them, who possess the means of breathing and of speaking to each other. A different type of wind is associated with each of the cardinal directions and is the means by which the inner forms communicate with the sky and those living on the earth's surface.[4] The mountain itself is often called a hogan or house in which many different beings, including animal and plant forms, may also reside. All of these may be appealed to through songs and prayers that were first used when the creation of the world and its processes began. A medicine man said,

> whenever anything was established for the use of the earth people, it required song and prayer. In that way [the gods] put it into motion; it became alive, just by the songs, the actions, and the prayers. Now with us, we cannot do that because we do not have the power to create anything. If we were singing, it would not come to life at all. But we can keep the power alive today by using those songs that were used when the first Blessingway was created.[5]

By learning the origin, songs, and prayers of a creation by the gods, one obtains the powers and privileges that accompany that knowledge.

The mountains have human qualities and personalities, based on the spiritual form that lives within. As with everything in the Navajo universe, these forms are paired as males and females. The sacred mountains of the west and south are female, and those to the east and north are male. Each one has a different personality and, like many of the holy beings, has its trials and triumphs. One story tells of how after the mountains were dressed in their respective clothing of white shell, turquoise, abalone, and jet, Mount Taylor went crazy and cut off her dress of turquoise and did strange things with her hair. The other mountains became upset and so the gods placed mountain tobacco on their slopes so that they could smoke the plant and settle down. The plan worked and the mountains have remained settled to this day.

This event is not taken lightly since young women today are doing the same thing—shortening their dresses, wearing pants, and curling their hair. If this continues, they too may go crazy and never reach the age of white hair as the mountains have, with snow on their summits. Mountain tobacco is still used to calm people with troubled minds and lustful thoughts.[6]

Sacred mountains should not be climbed unless it is done in a proper way through prayer and song, and they should be returned to by medicine men every twelve years to renew their Blessingway prayers. Frank Mitchell, a medicine man, told of visiting these mountains over a period of three years to collect dziłleezh, or mountain soil, for his earth bundle, used for healing and protection. When his group reached the mountain, they removed their regular clothes, purified themselves and their equipment, and sang songs during much of their journey. Once on top, the leader placed ntł'iz, a small offering comprised of corn pollen, white shell, turquoise, abalone, and jet, before removing the soil.[7] Used in most Navajo ceremonies, ntł'iz is an important gift to the holy people that incorporates the powers of the mountains with prayer.

Failure to follow correct procedure leads to either individual harm or the loss of powers of a sacred site. For instance, one informant said that it was dangerous to try to climb Blanca Peak without proper spiritual preparation because "the rocks slip from under you" and because it is guarded by lightning. He told of two men who tried to do it but were engulfed in a cloud where they could feel the electricity in their hair and hear it crackle.[8] Treating the sacred places on a mountain in sacrilegious ways, including mining, road construction, logging, ranching, and recreation, causes the holy beings to flee and their power to be lost.

The values associated with sacred mountains are pervasive in Navajo life. In every ceremony the powers of the mountains and their deities are invoked to render aid in healing the sick, protecting the people and their

Navajo Mountain is associated with many teachings, some of which can be discussed only during certain seasons. "Our stories of creation are very sacred. We cannot tell stories like these whenever or however we want because they are a 'shield' for our well-being. If we do not hold them sacred, we will be destroyed." Florence Norton, Montezuma Creek. *(Photo by author)*

goods, bringing rain for crops and livestock, and insuring tranquility in life. One man said that

> the white people all look to the government like we look to the sacred mountains. You . . . hold out your hands to the government. In accord with that, the government, you live. But we look to our sacred mountains. . . . According to them we live—they are our Washington (government).[9]

As mentioned previously, the mountains are said to be forked hogans of the gods, and so the hogan of the Diné replicates this pattern. The four main poles used in its construction represent the mountains, the ceiling is the sky, and the floor the desert lands. When blessing a hogan, the person praying sprinkles corn pollen on the four main posts and is said to be "dressing the mountains." Once the supernatural beings have been invited to witness the blessing of this structure, it becomes a suitable place for ceremonies to be held.[10]

The Navajo wedding basket also reflects many values of traditional life and so often contains all six sacred mountains, including Huerfano and Gobernador Knob, though the size of the basket may determine the number of mountains in the design. The center spot in the basket represents the beginning of this world, where the Navajo people emerged from a reed. This is where the spirit of the basket lives. The white part around the center is the earth, the black symbolizing the sacred mountains upon which are found water bowls. Above them are clouds of different colors. The white and black ones represent the making of rain. A red section next to the mountains stands for the sun's rays that make things grow.[11] Similar uses of a mountain motif are found in woven blankets, silverwork, sand paintings, and the Navajo tribal seal.

But what of those mountains near the Four Corners that are not among the four or six most sacred ones? To the people who live near them, they assume an important but subordinate role. These also have sacred places, an inner form, and a sexual identity, and most have stories that explain their creation. Understanding about a mountain or some other topographical feature depends heavily on the training and ceremonial knowledge of the informant.

What follows is a compilation of thoughts about places in the Four Corners region. Not all of the people interviewed agree upon certain aspects, but all express love and concern for the land from which they draw close religious and economic ties.

One of the most dramatic landforms in southern Utah is Navajo Mountain or Naatsis'áán—Head of Earth Woman. A number of mythological stories surround this region. One of the earliest tales concerns a supernatural being named Monster Slayer (Naayéé' Neizghání) who, with his brother, Born for Water (Tóbájíschíní), made the earth's surface safe for people. The twins' supernatural powers—derived from their father, the sun, and from their mother, Changing Woman—allowed them to kill monsters inhabiting the earth after the Diné's emergence from the worlds below.

During this process of cleansing the land, Monster Slayer went to the area of Navajo Mountain where an evil being called He Who Kicks People Off Monster (Tsé dah Hódziiłtáłii) lived. Monster Slayer walked on the narrow trail high upon the cliff where this being sat with his legs drawn up ready to kick. After four fruitless attempts to send the hero over the precipice, the monster innocently suggested that he was just trying to stretch his legs. Monster Slayer carved him up with his great knife, threw his body into the canyon, and then descended to the desert floor to kill the creature's twelve children. The last one was not destroyed because it was so ugly and dirty; instead it was sent to live in exile at Navajo Mountain because "it was a barren land, where you will have to work hard for a living, and will wander ever naked and hungry."[12] He was the progenitor of the Paiute people.

A more positive story tells how enemy gods on the San Francisco Peaks wanted to enslave Monster Slayer, who, according to local tradition, was born on Navajo Mountain. They fired projectiles tipped with spruce and juniper at him, which he caught and planted as trees on the slopes. Thus the mountain became a shield to the Navajo people, and during the trauma of Kit Carson and his Utes' forays into this country, the Diné hid in its recesses, invoking the power of Monster Slayer.[13] The main ceremonies performed today at Navajo Mountain are Protectionway and Blessingway, used to help soldiers during wars and to protect against hunger, evil power, and loss of livestock.[14]

Associated with this story are sacred sites on or near the mountain. Near the summit on the southern slope "there is a small area formed of black rocks in a semicircle," which is where Monster Slayer was born. Nearby is a sacred spring, where precipitation is formed and where offerings are made. A story tells of how the rain and clouds stood only at Navajo Mountain; and so, as other places started to dry out, the holy people sent a wind to blow the clouds into different areas.[15]

In hunting mythology, this area is mentioned as a place visited by

Black God, the keeper of game animals. He made this the home of all white-tailed deer, and from here they moved to other areas. They told Black God, "We are stationed here, and we travel by lightning. This is how we live. . . . In the future, as far as man is concerned, he may call us the White-streaked Ones."[16]

Another belief about Navajo Mountain ties in land formations that extend into northern Arizona and northwestern New Mexico. After the holy beings fashioned the six most sacred mountains, they had materials left over and so made eight more, which they named When the Mountains Get Finished They Get New Again. Some of these mountains comprise two figures, one male and one female, that lie in the desert as a pair of anthropomorphic forms. The head of the female is Navajo Mountain, her body is Black Mesa, her feet are Balukai Mesa, and El Capitán ('Aghaałą́, more commonly spelled Agathla Peak) is a wool twiner she is holding. Some Navajos also suggest that Comb Ridge is one arm, a monocline near Marsh Pass the other, and Tuba Butte and El Capitán are her breasts. The entire formation is known as Pollen Mountain. The male is identified as the Goods of Value Mountain. His head is Chuska Peak or Tohatchi Mountain, his body is the Chuska-Tunicha range, while his lower extremities are the Carrizo Mountains, with his feet located at Beautiful Mountain, New Mexico. He holds in one hand a bow or a sacred medicine pouch, which is Shiprock.[17] Some people suggest that these forms are lying together in a posture of mating, the male facing west and the female east. Others say that they "lie head to tail, and in that fashion the old men and womenfolk lie, with the head of one at the feet of the other. They (the mountains) say to each other, 'Your dirty feet are bothersome,' and so also say the old folks to one another."[18] Just as these beings are blessed with plants, animals, and rain and share these with humans, so too should people be loving and sharing with each other.

Once a man named Tall Bitter Water was asked to sign a paper that would open the Carrizo Mountains to mineral exploitation. He replied that the earth was his mother and then, referring specifically to this region, he said,

> The mountains have arms and legs and a head and everything. They are alive. . . . [The] Carrizo is the legs of these mountains. What is it going to stand on if we turn it over to you? How are we going to live? . . . How would you like to have anyone bother your legs? . . . If someone got everything out of your legs and your feet, how could you stand up? . . . This mountain is

our forefather. He is taking care of all the Navaho. He helps us to get the sick well and after he gets the people well we are happy again.[19]

As a separate entity, the Carrizo Mountains are known as Dził Náhoozիlii, meaning The Mountain That Gropes Around. From its slopes, Navajos collect herbs and plants and graze their livestock. One man indicated that it was one of the few mountains left that still had its "arms open" in welcome to the Diné.[20] Many mountains seem closed to Navajo use because of government control, but Forest Service policy does not indicate that this is the case.

To the northeast of the Carrizo Mountains lies Sleeping Ute Mountain or Dzil Naajini, translated as Black Mountain Sloping Down. This feature is fastened to the sky by a cord of rain; is decorated with corn pollen, dark mist, and female rain; and has Holy Boy and Holy Girl, who dwell within and make rough jewels.[21]

Most Navajos agree, however, that this mountain and its environs are Ute land, and they tell a story of how a Ute man died and asked to be buried there. Sticks and branches with leaves were placed on top of the body, which was laid to rest with head to the north, face toward the sky, arms across the chest, and thighs, knees, and toes to the south.

The Utes, on the other hand, believe this was one of their deities, who was angered by his people and so collected rain clouds, put them in his pocket, then went to sleep. When a storm arises, it is only the clouds coming out of the rain god's pocket. Some say that the Sleeping Ute will one day awake to fight his people's enemies.[22]

Blue Mountain is Dził Dítł'ooii, or Furry Mountain. It is a female with its paired male, Dzil 'Ashdla'ii (the La Sal Mountains), meaning The Five Mountains, to the north. Both ranges are noted for their medicinal plants, which will be discussed later. One man said, "It has sat there since the beginning of time with medicine. When the Navajo are going to have a ceremony, they always go over there . . . for cedar and yucca plants of various sizes."[23] A number of Navajos indicated that Blue Mountain produced a good breed of horses because of the horsehead figure made of trees on the east slope. This male figure is matched by a female horsehead on the west slope, though no specific location for this figure is given. Many mentioned that it was a good place to hunt deer, while in some mythology Blue Mountain was said to be covered with elk.[24]

Like all mountains, there is placed within life-giving water that comes from a bowl buried at its summit. Springs, rivers, and rain pour forth from this source, bringing clouds, vegetation, and animal life to the region. The tó 'asaa', or water bowl, is an important feature in an arid climate that depends on mountain storms and water for its moisture.[25]

Mountains serve yet another function. On top of the four sacred peaks are sky pillars (Yá Yíyah Niizíinii, or Those Who Stand under the Sky) that hold up the sky and the sun at a safe distance. Stories concerning these pillars conflict, but they generally agree that during the creative process Changing Woman lit a turquoise disk with a crystal and gave light and heat to man. The fiery object in the sky became too hot, and because the sky hung too close to the earth, a need arose to hoist both higher. Humans were sweltering from the extreme temperatures and could not stand upright because of the low-lying sky. First Man and First Woman were able to raise the sun a certain distance and then, with the help of twelve holy beings, raised it further. The men also stretched the earth by blowing, creating an even further distance from the sun. On the sacred mountains these men still hold the sky in position; others are spread throughout Navajo land. El Capitán is one that is located at the center of the world; Alhambra Rock at Mexican Hat is another.[26]

Thus, the land and its mountains were formed under the direction of the gods for the benefit of man. They embody some of the most powerful and important teachings within Navajo religion, while providing the physical means to sustain the people in a lifestyle highly dependent upon the resources that come from them.

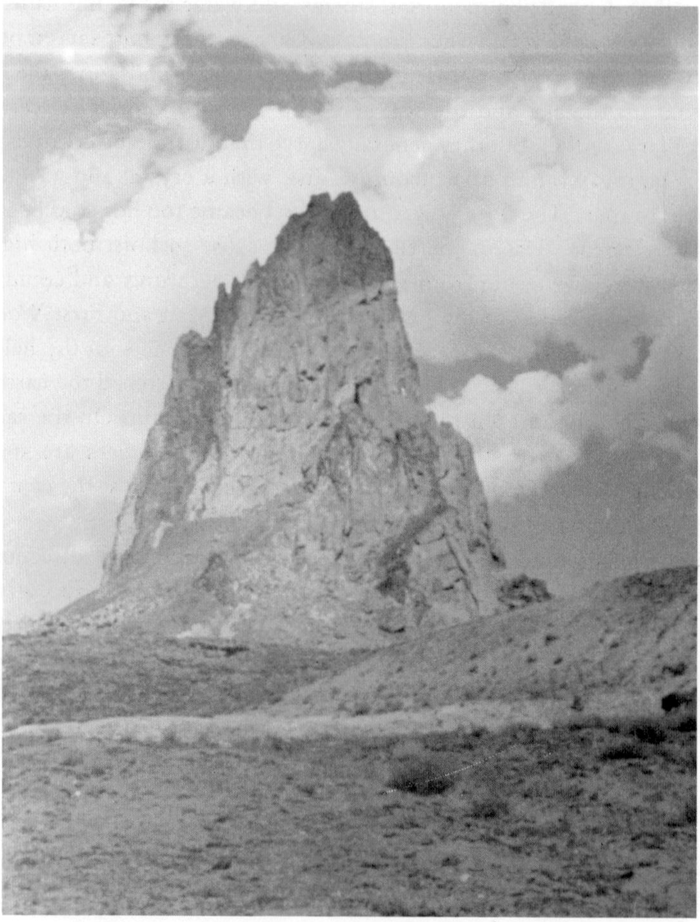

El Capitan is one of several sky-supporters in the area. Some older Navajos have also described it as a type of "transmitter" capable of communicating prayers to Jóhonaa'éí.
(Photo by author)

CHAPTER TWO

Rock Formations

Rock formations are also places of power in which spirits reside, and the formations in Valley of the Gods are some of the most distinctive. These imposing monoliths are Navajo warriors frozen in stone, who can be appealed to for protection. They are guardians whose power and strength aid young men going to war. By placing ntł'iz at the base of one of these pinnacles, one pleases the spirit inside, who will then provide supernatural help to the one whose name is mentioned or whose voice is heard in prayer. People are cautioned not to climb on these rocks for fear of offending the holy being and because one does not know to which clan or tribe these frozen warriors belong. Another prayer site for servicemen is located at the top of Long Mountain in the Shonto area. This is important to the people in the Tuba City, Navajo Mountain, Shonto, and Oljato areas.[1]

Not far from Valley of the Gods lies a series of rock formations important in Navajo beliefs. Lime Ridge has a trapezoidal block of sandstone that looks like a forked hogan. In it are trapped children who were disobedient to Jóhonaa'éí (Sun Bearer) and so are being punished. The story tells of how the god warned them not to steal animals and to be respectful of people's property, but they repeatedly failed to do his bidding. Jóhonaa'éí placed them in the hogan for four days, trying to bring them to repentance; but when this failed, the hogan turned to solid rock. When a person is near this site, he can hear them crying.[2]

Behind this rock lives a horned snake that is male, while on the eastern side of Lime Ridge is its mate. These two supernatural beings guard the eastern boundary to Navajo land that exists as a ledge across from the rock hogan. This ledge extends for over a mile down the valley. A perfectly square block is missing from this rock shelf, while a matching square is located several hundred meters away, perched on a mesa. A story tells of how one day, Coyote, the trickster, while walking along discouraged, scuffed his foot in disgust and knocked the rock out of the ledge and onto the hill, where it rests to this day.[3]

The Goosenecks of the San Juan River, described as the coils of a huge serpent (The One Who Crawls With Her Body), is one of a number of local geographic features associated with snakes. *(Photo by author)*

Mexican Hat is called Ch'ah łizhin, or Black Hat, and seems to have few stories associated with it. But behind this rock lies Mountain That Is Coiled (Dzil Na'neest'ee'i), also known as Navajo Blanket. The pattern on the hill reflects the same design of the giant bullsnake (díyóósh) that lives inside. People who have tried to uncoil this snake have been hissed at with large puffs of air. Bad luck accompanies those who trespass this area and do not show the proper respect. For instance, people have drowned in the river below, said to have been killed by the snake that slips down to the water. Big Snake can also wriggle over the ground without touching it and can harm a person mentally just by being present. When people disappear in this area, it is credited to the serpent; and when an oil company could not drill successfully at a site near here, it was because the snake kept pushing the drill bit out of the earth. Even white men have died here because of its power.

Many different kinds of snakes live here as kinds of representatives of Big Snake. The river is sometimes described as a large serpent, whose body is coiled at the Goosenecks. One person suggested that Big Snake received its nourishment by drawing it with a type of magnetic force from the Bears Ears, linking two of the most powerful and dangerous animals in Navajo religion, the bear and the snake, in geographical landforms.[4] Medicine men pray at this spot and say that beauty in the form of protection will come because they recognize this power. In the olden days, these men fashioned objects from carnotite for protection and placed them nearby.

To the south lies There Is a Treeless Area amid the Rocks, called by the white man Monument Valley. Various explanations exist about the De Chelly Sandstone monoliths that cover this region. For example, some say that the large monuments are barrels or Navajo water baskets. The seeps at their bases such as Sand Spring, Pine Tree Spring, and Bullsnake Spring are there for the people's use, thanks to the holy beings. Rain God Mesa has four springs located at its bottom in the four cardinal directions, and so medicine men collect water there for ceremonies associated with healing and rainmaking.[5] This mesa, and Thunderbird Mesa nearby, are the homes of thunder and lightning, whose powers are said to have caused the crash of a military aircraft that flew too low over the mesa. Other places, where streams of desert varnish mark the path of water over the edge of rocks, are also used to pray for water.

All of Monument Valley is a hogan. Its fireplace is the butte near Goulding's Trading Post and its door faces east near the Tribal Park

In the past, Totem Pole Rock in the Navajo Tribal Park has been an important site for rain-producing ceremonies. One man tells of going there in the midst of a drought and offering ntł'iz to the four directions. The rain arrived in earnest by the time he was halfway home, filling the washes and coursing down the rocks. *(Photo by Tom Austin)*

The Mittens are two of the most frequently photographed monoliths in the Navajo Tribal Park. Called "Big Hands," or barrels with spouts, these "female" formations have come to characterize the dramatic beauty of Navajo land. *(Photo by author)*

ranger station, Sentinel Mesa and Gray Whiskers Mesa being the doorposts. At Gray Whiskers Mesa, Eagle Mesa, and Mitchell Butte are water seeps at which earth bundles and prayers are offered. Many of these formations are also water barrels.

Nearby stands Totem Pole Rock, said by some to be a line of prayersticks and by others to be a frozen yé'ii, or god, held up by lightning. Because people have climbed on it, the spirit is offended and so now there is not as much rain in Monument Valley as there used to be. The rock is also said to be the dancing feathers used in the Mountainway ceremony, while underneath is the home of the mirage people (hadahoniye'), who have powers to bless and bring wealth to those who leave offerings there.[6]

The Mittens are two hands that lie dormant, left behind by the gods as signs that some day the holy beings will return and rule with power from Monument Valley. These rocks are also water barrels with pouring spouts. Eagle Mesa is a sacred place, to which the spirit of a dead person goes after burial. One can hear the voices of babies and adults in this area and can see their bones and footprints on the mesa. The tops of all the mesas that align between Douglas Mesa and the Bears Ears form a pathway walked by the holy beings during their travels.[7] Many of the single monoliths are holy people frozen in form.

> The Stagecoach and the Bear and Rabbit are Yé'ii Bicheíí dancers. The adjacent rock (part of Castle Butte) and the Big Indian are dancers that circle the ye'iis; the Big Indian is the clown (water sprinkler) with a coyote skin and the other of the pair wears a buckskin. The two-pronged King on His Throne comprises two leaders. The Three Sisters are three holy people who were turned to stone.[8]

Igneous rocks are usually associated with supernatural events and powers. Alhambra Rock is not only a sky supporter but also a group of holy beings performing a ye'ii bichei dance. El Capitán, or Agathla, another sky supporter, is called Much Wool and is said to be like a transmitter that beams information to the sun or to White Shell Woman, who lives near the ocean.[9]

Two different stories are associated with Agathla. The first goes back to the period of creation when the land was soft and creatures talked and acted like humans. The animals started on a journey from Navajo Mountain. Big Snake, who is endless, traveled with the others until they reached the area of Agathla. He complained of how tired he was and urged the

Comb Ridge, among other things, is described as one of four arrowheads used during the creative period to carve the earth. Other "arrowheads" are found near Albuquerque, Denver, and Moab. The major rivers near these cities were created by the waters that once covered the land but have since seeped into these furrows. (See pages 36–37.) *(Photo by Stan Byrd)*

group to eat and camp there. The next day, when it was time to depart, Big Snake said all this movement had worn his stomach raw and he could go no further, and so he stayed behind as the others continued their journey. Prior to leaving, however, the group made a hole for him as he curled around the rock before descending into his new home. His wife, the owl, said by others to be a homosexual, remained with her husband and still sits to the west of his home. Deer and antelope were plentiful, and the serpent had no trouble luring them to his abode, where he ate them and piled their fur outside. Thus the legend explains why the name of Much Wool is tied to this rock, as well as why snakeskin is still found in crevices on or near the formation.[10]

Another story from the Bead Chant tells of how the Two Came for the Water clan joined the Western Water clans at this place. The rock received its name from deer hair scraped off the hides in the tanning process. Some people say that it has a stepladder leading up to a place where wool used to be stored in its recesses, while others suggest the rock is a wool-twirling tool.[11]

Many miles to the east of El Capitán is another igneous intrusion called Tsidił, or Stick Dice. Old women were gambling there day and night until they died from of old age. Their dice remain, while their bodies rest in their home, a neighboring hill. These rocks may also be k'eet'áán s, or prayersticks.[12]

Another prayerstick, this one of sandstone, is in Bluff. The Navajo Twins are a familiar landmark to people passing through Cow Canyon, but few realize that these rocks represent the sacred materials that comprise a k'eet'áán. Their elements may include white shell, turquoise, abalone, jet, bluebird feathers, eagle and turkey down, mountain tobacco, and the colors associated with the four directions. The layers on the Navajo Twins represent these objects, and when the Diné leave prayers and offerings in the vicinity, they may be blessed with twin children.[13]

Other well-known sites also hold power. Karl Luckert has documented the beliefs surrounding Rainbow Bridge near Navajo Mountain, which include the idea that the arch is comprised of two beings—one male, one female—stretched across the canyon together. From their union come the rain people, rainbows, clouds, and moisture that originate here and spread over the reservation. These beings in the arch work in concert with the sacred sites on Navajo Mountain and the meeting place of the Colorado and San Juan rivers.[14]

Rainbow Bridge is also a frozen rainbow by which supernatural people traveled. Two women walked away from Black Water and arrived at this location, where they met the holy people. They requested to stay with the supernaturals, but this was denied. However, they were given a means by which they could return to their people—a rainbow arch that became frozen in form. To walk under the arch is impolite since no one can walk under a real rainbow. Because of the increased tourism at this site and the rising waters of Lake Powell, rituals are no longer possible here. The holy beings require that the ceremony be performed during the day, in a solemn, quiet manner. Speedboats and tourists "looking over one's shoulder" preclude such sacred communication.[15]

Just as these are places of sacred, beneficial power, there are also sites where witchcraft and evil powers are prominent. Informants are reluctant to discuss this side of Navajo culture, but Black Mesa near Kayenta is an area where witchcraft appears to be powerful. Caves or cracks in the rocks may be entrances that open into an 'áńt'įį́ bahoogan, or witch's home. Incest, the murder of close relatives, the making of corpse poison, and witches' sabbaths may take place in these rooms, which are inaccessible to regular humans from the outside.

Skinwalkers, or humans who control supernatural evil, are said to travel a route (near Sand Island bridge) which passes by the white-tipped bluffs on the way to a place where the San Juan joins a side canyon stream and on to a home for the practitioners of evil.[16]

A few miles from this trail lies Tsénąąshch'aa'i, or Designs on the Rock. On one side of the top of the rocks is a thin, flat ridge where witching practices are held. Another site is called Tsézhiin'íí'áhí, or Standing Black Rock, and has strong powers within it to be used against people. The rock is witched and can cause starvation.[17]

Rock and land formations also help to tell the future. In Monument Valley there is a rock with white coloration on the cliff behind Goulding's Trading Post which serves as a warning to the Diné. When it falls, something bad will happen, like the death of an important person, an illness, or a natural calamity. Chaistla Butte near Kayenta will fall down when the end of the world arrives. This is also true of other places, where rocks break off from a cliff face to give warning of impending disaster.

Apparent proof of these beliefs occurred in 1987 when a rockslide south of Goulding's Post went unheeded. No prayers were said, no ceremonies were performed—and soon a gang of men confronted and killed two Navajo policemen in the area. In the 1960s Frank Mitchell, from another part of the reservation, believed that a war was going to start soon. He said, "I can tell because of the way the rocks are starting to split in the canyon. We saw them when we went in there recently. It is just the way they were splitting before the beginning of the last world war."[18] Soon the Vietnam War erupted.

Another site is now covered by the waters above Navajo Dam, near Farmington, New Mexico. Called the Shining Sands, it was located at the Meeting Place of Waters. Medicine men went there only occasionally when general events indicated a dramatic change. The singers purified themselves and moved to the junction of the rivers, where a small sandbar was submerged under a shallow covering of water. They left offerings of ntł'iz, sang and prayed all night, then returned the next day to read the ripples in the sand. Forecasts presaged events after Bosque Redondo in 1868, again in 1929 just before livestock reduction, and one other time before the dam backed up the water. This last reading indicated heavy rains, a journey to distant places, wind, lightning, floods, and crossed sticks that marked a burial—an ominous portent of things to come.[19]

Shiprock and the Bears Ears are two sites that fit into the major ceremonial lore. The first one, Shiprock (Tsé̩ Bit'ą'í), is in New Mexico. Stories vary but revolve around the central figure of Monster Slayer, who received lightning arrows from Jóhonaa'éí to destroy the monsters killing the Diné. One such creature was Deelgeed, who murdered people with his breath and then ate them. He was destroyed at Red Mesa, staining the sands red with his blood.[20] Monster Slayer took his intestines and blood and started to Shiprock, where two large monster birds, called tsé'náhalééh, lived high on a flat area of the rock. These birds killed their prey by smashing them on the rocks and letting their young feast on the remains. When the tsé'náhalééh picked up the hero twin and dropped him, he landed lightly because of a life feather given him by Spider Woman. He dashed the intestines on the rocks to make it appear as though he had died, then asked the two young tsé'náhalééh when their parents would return. They replied that the father came back when male rain and lightning appeared, the mother when female rain occurred. Before long the male returned, and Monster Slayer shot him down with lightning arrows. He next destroyed the female.

Then the young started to cry, asking if they too would be destroyed, to which Monster Slayer replied, "Had you grown up here you would have been things of evil; you would have lived only to destroy my people; but I shall now make of you something that will be used in the days to come

Bears Ears, a noted landmark to travelers in southeastern Utah, appeared on Spanish maps as early as the 1700s. These formations hold many medicinal plants and play a role in ceremonies to relieve depression. *(Photo by author)*

when men increase in the land."[21] Swinging the older one around four times, he directed that it should furnish plumes and bones for the use of men. The bird soared away as an eagle. The Twin gave the younger one the same treatment, saying that men would listen to its voice to learn the future. The bird flew off as an owl.

Rabbit, who was down below, took feathers from the dead tsé'náhalééh and stuck them in his fur, and that is why jackrabbits look like they have feathers for ears. After spending four days on the rock, Monster Slayer received help from Bat Woman, who provided her burden basket for the hero to descend in. He then returned to Born for Water and camped near the junction of Mancos Creek and the San Juan River.[22]

Shiprock, until recently, was sacred. From this story comes part of the Enemyway ceremony, which specifies rituals for protection and sacred sites with power. Monster Slayer made the world safe from his enemies, while Born for Water performed the necessary rites of protection at home. Warriors today reenact and are protected by similar supernatural events, provided by recreating the actions through ceremonial performances. Medicine men still copy the Twins by placing ntł'iz on the highest peaks, at a lightning-struck tree, and in the San Juan River. However, Shiprock could never be used this way again after a Sierra Club climbing party profaned it in 1939.[23]

One of the most powerful symbols of protection and the battle of good over evil lies in the Bears Ears, west of Blanding. Stories associated with this landmark capture the importance of power, prayers, and protection and serve as a mnemonic device in the landscape to warn against treachery, deceit, and cunning. Teachings surrounding the Bears Ears continue to play a central part in Navajo beliefs.[24]

The story starts with a beautiful young woman who refused wedlock to many suitors. She lived with her twelve brothers, kept a neat home, and had a decorous life. One day, Coyote wandered into camp and asked her to marry him, but she gave him a series of challenges to overcome before she would accept. Through trickery and magic, he completed his tests, though both the girl and her brothers wished that he had failed. The woman kept her word, married Coyote, and started to learn his devious ways and evil knowledge. The brothers took him hunting but felt no love for their in-law, who wandered off to a series of adventures and mishaps. The woman, however, had been contaminated. She assumed the qualities of evil, disorder, and the ability to change into a bear—hence her name, Changing Bear Maiden.

Her brothers became increasingly concerned about the strange behavior of their sister, and so they sent the youngest boy to spy on her. He watched as she secretly assumed the qualities of a bear through ritual behavior. She faced the four directions, pulled out her eyeteeth, and inserted bone awls in their stead. Hair spread over her body, her ears wagged, her snout grew longer, her nails turned to claws, and her teeth made a fearful gnashing noise. The youngest brother reported what he had seen to his brothers, who then chose to remain at home.

For four days the sister went in search of her missing husband, who had failed to return. Her anger was taken out on those she met. Each time she returned home with arrows stuck in her flesh from the enemies she fought, and each time she shook them out of her body.

When her brothers left to the four directions to go hunting, she methodically tracked them down and killed them all, except for the youngest one, who was hidden in a hole in the ground covered over by rocks and dirt. The Wind (níłch'i) served as his guardian. Changing Bear Maiden returned to her camp in search of the sole survivor. She excreted on the ground, saying that whichever direction her stool fell or her urine ran, that was where she would find her brother. It just stood up straight and puddled, so she dug down, found her brother, and then offered to help comb his hair and get him cleaned up.

Wind warned that he should sit so that the sun would cast a shadow of his sister that he could watch. Just before she bent close to him for the fifth time, he sprang to his feet, ran to a bush where she had hidden her vital organs, and let fly a lightning arrow. Blood gushed forth from the bush as well as the bear. Wind warned that if the two separate streams of blood should meet, she would revive and be even harder to kill and so the brother took a knife and made a deep furrow to keep the liquids apart.

He next addressed the body and said, "You shall live again but no longer as the mischievous bear-woman. You shall live in other forms, where you may be of service to your kind and not a thing of evil." He cut off her vagina and tossed it up into a tree, where it became a porcupine. He did the same with the left nipple, and it became piñon nuts; the right one became acorns, the glands within the breast yucca fruit, and her entrails sorrel, dock, and other plants. Her paunch he dragged to the water, which became alkali, while her limbs became various types of bears which he sent off with a strict warning to behave. The head, which he threw away, is now the Bears Ears, while the furrow dug with his knife is Comb

Ridge and Wash.[25] By these actions good triumphed over evil, and the slain brothers came back to life.

This story illustrates important values in Navajo culture. The woman changed from a respected and talented girl to the height of evil, killing family members and losing control of her human faculties. Impurity, filth, and disorder became her way of life, and Coyote dominated her thoughts and actions.[26] One of the Evilway Chants, called Upward Reaching Way, recounts this story, with destruction of evil and pain as a central theme. Patients who have evil dreams reenact the events played out in the story in order to be cured.

Changing Bear Maiden is often responsible for mental illness. For instance, "when a person loses his mind or becomes insane . . . [or starts to] rattle the teeth or gnash them," a figurine of her, as well as prayersticks, are carved and placed with offerings at a sacred site.[27] If one walks or sleeps where a bear has been, gets ants on him that have been on a bear, uses brush cut by a bear, drinks at its watering place, steps on its tracks, or talks or dreams of one, that person's hearing may be affected or he may become weak. Ceremonies are required to rectify the situation.[28] Because of this story, plants used to cure witchcraft and incest are picked on the Bears Ears. Once gathered, they are crushed and sprinkled around the home in a clockwise manner, the person being careful never to complete the circle and trap the evil in.[29] Since Coyote was the one who helped bring about the death and destruction, when a coyote howls near a home it means that death will come to the family living there.[30]

The Bears Ears is also viewed as a male guardian, one of a pair, that protects Dibé' Ntsaa. The female counterpart is located in the Carrizo Mountains, though no exact location has been specified. Bears as paired guardians are a common motif in the sand paintings of the Mountainway, where they protect an entrance from evil influences.[31] Bears and arrowheads are often used in ceremonies to represent protection and armor applied to the patient. Florence Begay explains:

> When the two [bears] are brought together, they take care of the mountain. For this reason, they have the Shashchiin—miniature bears made out of special stones such as turquoise and jet, which are used when prayers are offered. The ones who have these are the ones who hold special prayers to ward off evil. . . . It is like this within the Navajo boundaries. The bear is standing to guard and another bear is guarding the opposite side. For that reason, when a prayer is being offered, there is a part that says that the

> Great Dark Black Bear will stand guard, you will walk to protect or shield me.[32]

A different-colored bear may be called from each of the directions, bringing with it flint points to keep harm away from the patient.[33]

This motif of the bear as protector is found in other narratives. One story tells of a supernatural bear who took pity on the Diné because they were constantly defeated by their enemies. The bear performed certain rituals, sang prescribed songs, and then went out and wreaked havoc on invading war parties. When the enemy was destroyed, the bear took plants and arrowheads and placed them in the ground as he sang:

> I make a mark, they won't cross it.
> Monster Slayer I am, they won't cross it.
> . . . .
> Black obsidian zigzag lightning darts four times from me stream out.
> Where it goes dangerous missiles will be scattered.
> I make a mark they won't cross.
> I come back with lightning streaming out from me in four places.
> I come back, dangerous things and missiles being scattered.[34]

Thus the number four, concentric barriers, arrowheads, and the bear combine to make a powerful protective force behind which the Diné can live free from fear.

Comb Ridge, in addition to being the furrow dug by the youngest brother, is also described as one of four arrowheads that help protect Navajo land. The ridge is made of points set upright, which comprise one main arrowhead that extends to Blanding. The Diné call the ridge Tse'k'aan, or Rocks Standing Up. It is also called the backbone or spine of the earth and is believed to go into the ground and around the world. One person referred to it as Big Snake, with its tail toward Kayenta. This snake is feared and is associated with witchcraft brought up from the underworld.[35]

The Female Mountainway tells the story of two sisters who visited various locations in their quest to find each other. One woman wandered over to the Bears Ears and spent the night. There she met some bears, played with them, and then sat upon the bluff and sang a song of loneliness. The next day she moved on, but her example is still followed today. When a patient suffers from loneliness, sadness, or excessive weight loss, a medicine man may bring the person to the Bears Ears, where songs of comfort are sung. Before and after a Blessingway ceremony, people may go there for a short prayer and to dispose of yucca suds and materials from sand paintings.[36]

The Bears Ears also play an important part in Navajo history. The earliest dated hogan ring north of the San Juan River is in White Canyon, west of the Bears Ears. In 1801, Kaa'yeełii was born on Elk Ridge and his brother, Manuelito, was born shortly after. During the trauma of the 1860s, Kaa'yeelii established a camp with five or six hogans in a canyon called Naahootso, Place across the River to Escape from the Enemy, near the site of the ranger station at Kigalia Spring.[37] Here he avoided the general roundup of Navajos by Kit Carson and his Ute surrogates.

The canyon was a hiding place and the Bears Ears a prominent feature. Some Navajos suggest that it was a boundary between Ute and Navajo holdings, though in reality it was more likely a general-use area established in later times. The boundary passed between the ears and extended down Comb Ridge to Oljato; everything west of that line was Navajo and everything east was enemy.[38] This boundary passes by the serpent guards on Lime Ridge mentioned earlier.

Even in Navajo mythology the close proximity of the Utes to the Bears Ears, Allen Canyon, and Hammond Canyon is recognized. The wandering sister in search of her kin tells others: "That point extending is called Bears Ears. It is the Utes' Mountain. Have care not to go there." And later when two holy beings visit this place they comment, "We went around on Bears Ears to the home of the earth surface people. Their language was very abusive; earth surface people have no regard for holy things, that is evident."[39] This probably referred to the Utes in the area, since the Diné knew how to show proper respect.

The rock formations of the Four Corners region speak to the values of the Navajo people through their mythology. By tying supernatural events to geographical locations, the Diné imbue the land with sacred meaning and create a world of holiness. The stories teach of right and wrong, good and evil, reward and betrayal, all of which may be recreated by performing ceremonies at the locations where representative events occurred during mythological times. The land is filled with power that can be obtained through prayer for protection.

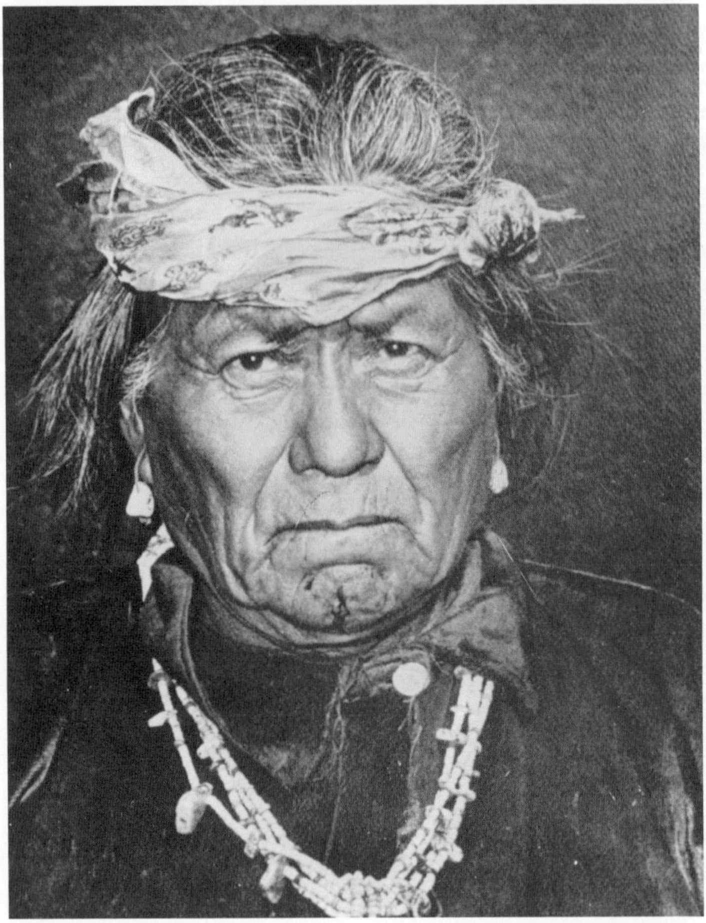

Hastiin Tso, a medicine man from Monument Valley, was noted for his ability to control the weather. John Ford, when directing movies on location, paid Hastiin Tso to provide appropriate weather for each day's filming. Witnesses say that the director was rarely disappointed.
(Photo courtesy San Juan County Historical Commission)

CHAPTER THREE

Earth and Sky

The relationship between the sky, the sun, and the earth is one of compatibility. The earth is female, the sky is male, and both meet as man and wife. The physical sun should not be confused with the deity Jóhonaa'éí, the Sun Bearer, who moves across the heavens on his daily trek, carrying the fiery orb. He is a powerful god, noted for his handsomeness, power, and progeny: the Twins, known as Monster Slayer and Born for Water.[1] His travels start in the east, because during the creative period the Wind of the East asked that he start from his edge of the world. Both Jóhonaa'éí and the moon bearer (Tłéhonaa'éí, Bearer of the Night) travel across the sky on one of thirty-two trails that range between the limits of the winter and summer solstices.[2]

The sun plays an active role in providing omens by which the Diné must live, while the moon does the same for the non-Navajo peoples. When the sun hides his light from the people because of his anger, he warns that a catastrophe will soon take place. Some people suggest that an eclipse is actually the death of the sun and that songs called Making the Sun Again (Jóhonaa'éí ánalyaa) help revive it. During an eclipse, ceremonies cease, people are awakened, and silence is maintained until the sun or moon "recovers."[3]

An example of how these heavenly bodies can presage misfortune is exemplified by the solar eclipse of June 8, 1918. During the following summer and fall, dawns and sunsets had pronounced reddish hues that bathed the landscape in an ominous red. The tips of cedar and juniper trees started to die, a sign indicating that sickness was in the area and would visit humans, while some Navajos had bad dreams portending disaster. Informants indicate that the holy beings sent the influenza epidemic, which brought death throughout the world that year, in order to make room for a growing population of young people; others suggest that poison gas or smoke and fumes from artillery rounds fired in the war in Europe somehow infected the people. Whatever the reason, the Diné were ill prepared for the ensuing sickness; thousands died during the fall and winter.[4]

Stars, though not as powerful as the sun, also have their teachings. When Black God, First Man, and First Woman started to place the stars in the heavens, they employed a fixed plan by which people could tell time, age, and era. Winter and summer celestial patterns had stars that led the other stars in their part of the universe. Big Star had five points and controlled the winter pattern, while 'Átsé'etsoh (Scorpius), led the summer groups. As the holy beings carefully positioned the heavenly bodies, they wondered what could be done with the remaining ones lying on a blanket at their feet. Coyote, the trickster, frustrated because they did not listen to his suggestions, grabbed the blanket and flung the stars upward, explaining, "What else can one do?" Thus there are constellations arranged in patterns as well as stars placed haphazardly in the evening sky.[5]

Just as most things in the Navajo universe reflect sexual duality, so do the stars. The Big Dipper is called Male Revolving One, who sits before a fire (Polaris, the North Star) and watches Revolving Female (Cassiopeia) as they move about the fire during the seasons. The Pleiades are seven boys who run and dodge as they practice shooting arrows, Corvus is a man with legs spread apart, and the tail of Scorpius is called Rabbit Tracks.[6]

The earth is the most important of the living celestial deities. Considered a female, she is often equated with Changing Woman, a beneficent holy being who embodies the mystery of birth and growth in nature. Her responsibility is to provide food for her people, gentle rain for their crops, assistance in reproduction, and peace in a world of strife. From her home near the ocean to the west, she oversees the changing seasons and urges her people to live well. "Pray with me, keeping me holy. Through that shall you live beautifully, my children."[7]

Changing Woman, like any mother, can be hurt by the misconduct of her children. She must be honored, and her offspring that walk upon Earth Mother must treat the land and each other with respect. People should not tell lies before their mother or cheat, steal, or cause harm. The Diné become sick upon entering mines that burrow beneath the earth's surface unless they say prayers of protection. The cancer found in many Navajos involved in uranium mining during the 1950s and 1960s occurred because of the lack of reverence shown to the earth as a living entity.[8] The rivers and streams are her veins; and they, like the rain, can diminish if respect is not shown. Navajo Oshley, a long-time resident of San Juan County, explained why one summer the rain decreased, the springs dried up, and the crops failed. He placed the blame on white men who did not understand what they were doing to the earth.

> People took up the land where the water was flowing and I have heard these people got stingy with the water.... This thing called water is for everything that is living, like horses and the birds. These people in Blanding say that the water is to be paid for. I do not like this.... That is why there is no rain.... There is the earth; we live on this and the Anglos are doing all sorts of things to it. They drill into the earth, and the Mormons do not take the sacredness of the land seriously and they are ruthless towards the land.... This causes the drought. They are digging into Mother Earth for minerals.... If they practiced the sacred ways, we would have rain and snow. They should offer prayers instead of drilling into Mother Earth.[9]

Since rain plays such an important role in Navajo life, a complex knowledge surrounds it. Clouds are classified as either female (light, puffy cirrus or cumulus clouds) or male (dark, heavy cumulonimbus clouds that cover much of the sky). Rain is also male or female. Male rain arrives in a downpour that scours the ground and runs in rivulets over the land and into the canyons. It is torrential rain, accompanied by jagged lightning, rumbling thunder, and destructive power. Where the lightning strikes is sacred and a sign of mighty supernatural power. Objects struck by male lightning are avoided unless a medicine man ritually protects himself from this power of the holy beings. Once this is done, however, he can use the power from a lightning-struck object or site to heal. Dead snakes come back to life when there is thunder and lightning, the latter often being compared to this reptile. Female rain, on the other hand, is accompanied by heat lightning and is a gentle, soaking shower that nurtures crops and lingers over the earth.

Ceremonies to obtain rain are important. Sacred springs, water seeps, river junctions, hilltops, mountaintops, rock arches, Anasazi ruins, water basins, and cliff bases where water pours over the rim all qualify as possible sites to place ntł'iz and pray to the holy beings for rain. Anasazi ruins may have a tó' asaa', or water bowl, planted in them to which ceremonial appeals from the Blessingway may be made. The medicine man performing the rite covers himself with white clay; as he returns from his prayers, the rain is said to wash off his markings. Cottonwood and willow limbs can also be suspended upside down on the posts of a male forked hogan to attract rain. However, because many people have forgotten these ceremonies, there is no longer the abundance of rain that there used to be.[10]

The Diné constantly search for indications that storms are approaching and that things are well with the holy beings. Good signs include rainbows around the sun, a sun dog (the atmospheric parhelion effect, called shá bitł'ájiiłchii' by the Diné), dampness in the air, a hazy horizon in the morning, and a north wind.[11] Rainbows are also classified according to sex, the male being a long, expansive arch and the female a short incomplete form. Those that go from east to west are male, and those that go from north to south are female.[12] Thus the male/female dichotomy pervades the universe.

A cloud having streamers of rain and mist suspended below as it floats over the land is said to represent the loosened hair of a person in a ceremony who has removed the traditional hair bun as a symbol of humility and prayer, and as a plea for rain in the presence of the gods. When it rains, a person should not stand in it, be in an open area, or carry guns and knives; rather, he should remove his weapons, sit down, be quiet, and maintain a reverent, quiet mood. This observance of proper behavior is pleasing to the holy beings as witnessed by the clouds.[13]

Hummingbirds also help obtain moisture. A long time ago, when the earth was parched, the animals held a meeting to pray for rain. The hummingbird attended but flew in and out, returning with water and water-related plants. The mouse said he knew where the bird flew, encouraged him to share his understanding, and helped bring rain to the area around the Bears Ears. From that time to the present, the hummingbird and mouse have worked as a pair to attract water to the land.[14]

Winter snows are also welcomed, though, as with rain and other things in nature — including humans — they have both a beneficial and a destructive side. Snow can cause avalanches, erosion, and death or can soak into the soil to nourish plants and other forms of life. One man compared this dichotomy to the human body, the left side of which is male, is aggressive, and holds the bow or arrowheads in a ceremony, while the right side is female and holds corn pollen, a symbol of life and peace. Both serve as checks and balances to each other, as do earth and sky, north and south, east and west, hunting and agriculture, Holyway and Evilway, and Blessingway and Enemyway. Winter snows are just one more illustration of the need for balance in nature and man. As the end of the world approaches, weather will reflect the oncoming doom. Thunder in the winter and snow in the summer will show that the holy beings are upset.[15]

Many stories told on winter evenings explain why the weather assumes its characteristics. Louisa Wetherill, when she lived in Oljato, learned the story of the woman who went among the Diné, stealing husbands from the wives. Her own husband tried to stop this by cutting off a part of her nose each time she was unfaithful, but to no avail. Finally the people held a ceremony and skinned her alive but could not kill her. She appeared before them clothed in cold, windy clouds and wearing a hat of ice. The woman went to the north, where she sits under the Little Dipper, and when she turns her face in anger she sends snow and cold to freeze the people.[16]

Another story tells of a person who found some burning material that he wanted to keep, but the gods forbade this. After the holy beings had him pass a series of tests, they agreed to give him all of the ashes from their fireplaces by dumping them in Montezuma Canyon, the place where the narrator of the story lived. Some years the gods forget to put any ashes or snow there, while at other times they put too much.[17]

The Diné say that the north is male because of the cold, violent winds (níyol) that come from Colorado, where mountain peaks dominate the landscape. Gentler winds and storms come from the south, in Arizona and New Mexico, a region where the mountains are less high and more female in their characteristics.

First Man initially placed the winds in the different directions and gave them the colors of spotted or white (east), blue (south), yellow (west), and black (north). These winds are accompanied by clouds reflecting the colors and qualities of the directions, such as dark thunderclouds and storms (north), yellow clouds with warm rain and weather (west), and blue skies and calm weather (south). The Diné also classify winds according to elevation: those found in flat areas and in high places, both of which may be strong or gentle.

Certain rock formations and sites where echoes are heard are the homes of wind, as are the circular bowls in rocks, and are places that should not be entered. Little holes in sandstone formations carved by the whirling spirit are the wind's footsteps. When it appears as a twister, it is sacred if it spirals clockwise, and has an evil spirit if it moves counterclockwise. Some Navajos believe that the northern end of Black Mesa serves as a funnel to prevent harmful winds from bothering other parts of the reservation. In addition to this protective, sacred mesa, there are also powerful medicine men who ceremonially encourage the winds to go by.[18]

Hilda Wetherill, who lived at a trading post at Covered Water, Arizona, recorded an example of the use of this type of power. One day a medicine man saw a twister headed directly for the store. Making gestures as if he were throwing kisses with both hands and pushing away with outstretched arms, he caused the wind to veer a mile and a half away from the post. Onlookers were amazed at the force of the wind and this man's ability to divert what seemed inevitable.[19]

To protect their crops from hot sandstorm winds that tear or shrivel corn and bean plants, in times past the Diné used to play two games. Kick-stick was performed by kicking two painted sticks around a ceremonial circuit on the outskirts of a planted field, while ball-race used a wooden or stone ball for the same purpose. Both of these games provided magical protection by pleasing the gods associated with crops.[20]

One of the most powerful forces that communicates between the elements of nature is that of another type of wind (níłch'i), a spiritual essence that pervades nature. Indeed, every living thing is touched by and communicates through níłch'i. One of its main functions is to give life and motion to plants, animals, and objects in the universe. That is why, in humans, hair curls out of the body's pores, hair swirls in a cowlick on top of the head, and prints on the hands and feet have circular patterns. The life wind within gives these forms to humans. The Diné are specific in pointing out that a baby in the fourth month of conception receives its wind, so that the body can grow until it is born. After birth, life continues because of the wind "that within us stands from our mouth downwards. . . . We breathe by it. It moves absolutely all of our blood vessels; it moves all parts of our body. We live by it."[21]

Wind also operates in all natural phenomena. For instance, the earth and the sky one time became angry with one another, each trying to claim its own self-importance. The wind came and settled the differences. It also communicates between the holy beings and their creations—the plants, animals, rocks, and the like.[22]

Surrounding all of these natural phenomena is a system of taboos to insure proper respect. The list is endless, so only a few are mentioned here. If a person points at a rainbow, his fingers will be broken or filled with pus. He should not look at clouds moving in the sky because he will be a slow runner. If he eats during an eclipse, his stomach will have trouble; and if he sleeps during one, he will be blind. One should not hold his hand out when it is snowing because where the hand is indicates how deep the snow will be.[23]

All of these ideas speak of the sacredness of nature, while serving as a constant reminder of man's dependence on supernatural help and the pleasure of the holy beings. To risk disfavor is to risk sickness, poverty, and death. In a land where weather spells the difference between good crops and poor yields, healthy sheep and decimated flocks, and survival and destruction, the Diné place an important value on the weather in its many forms.

The San Juan River serves as a boundary between the female side (south) and the male side (north). Religious beliefs forbid hunters to bring a deer south of the river without cutting off its skin and legs. "For if you do this, many of the foreign people will cross into your territory and take your land without hesitation. This has happened because we did the forbidden." John Holiday, medicine man, Monument Valley.
(Photo by Stan Byrd)

CHAPTER FOUR

Rivers and Streams

Another powerful force in the universe is the river. Like the sacred mountains that bound Navajo territory, there are four potent rivers inhabited by holy beings who answer prayers and provide protection. Everything within the boundaries of the Rio Grande, San Juan, Colorado, and Little Colorado rivers is protected and sacred, but that which extends beyond these limits is foreign and dangerous.

The Colorado River, a female called Life without End, and the Little Colorado, a male, served as a protective barrier for Changing Woman during the creative period. As she traveled with her animals, who served as helpers, she decided to rest one night in the area where the two rivers meet, not far from Tuba City. Once she fenced her companions in with the river boundaries, she made camp by the water. There she met a man, was seduced, and the next morning started to menstruate, the first Navajo person to do so. Before leaving, she washed the blood away in the river, making the water of the Little Colorado red, and left behind salt, turquoise, and various colored shells and beads for her lover. These elements can still be found there today.[1]

The most important of these rivers is the San Juan, known by various names as Old Age River (Są́ Bitooh), Male Water (Tooh Bikąʼi), One with a Long Body (Bitsʼíísnineezí), and One with a Wide Body (Bitsʼíínteelí). The Rio Grande and the Colorado are female rivers, or tóʼbáád, while the Little Colorado is male; they also have their ceremonial names.[2]

The San Juan is a powerful river described as an older man with hair of white foam, as a snake wriggling through the desert, as a flash of lightning, and as a black club of protection to keep invaders from Navajo lands. Within it is a holy being who married a female, the Colorado River, and, where these two spirits joined in nuptial bliss, they created water children of the cloud and rain people. Before Lake Powell covered their bed, the male San Juan actually mounted his mate, giving rise to a place for moisture-producing ceremonies.[3]

The holy being within the river has served as a guardian for a long time. As early as 1865, Manuelito claimed that he could not surrender to General James Carleton at Fort Sumner because "there was a tradition that his people should never cross the Rio Grande, Rio San Juan, or the Rio Colorado," and that he would remain where he was to "suffer all the consequences of war and famine."[4]

Today this protection is still in force. When older people cross the river, they sprinkle corn pollen to the holy being and ask for safety in their journey and accomplishment of their goals. The spirit hears the plea and wraps its power around them like a shield or rainbow. After the prayer, the speaker can step into the land of aliens — Utes or white men, for example — with impunity. In the past this was associated with dangerous activities such as warfare or hunting; now it is to trade or shop. Since most young people no longer show this type of respect and forget their prayers and pollen, the waters destroy them through pollution.[5]

Because the San Juan served as a geographical boundary for hunting expeditions and war parties, certain observances came into play when they crossed the river. For instance, Blessingway ceremonies for protection pertain to events and places within this area, while beyond the Colorado and San Juan rivers Enemyway and Evilway apply. The stick used in the Enemyway embodies many of the values important to the Navajo people and should never cross the river. Now that many Navajos live north of the San Juan, these proscriptions are no longer observed.

In the past, once the members of a hunting group or war party said their prayers and crossed the river, their actions changed. The warriors used a different language associated with fighting and killing, and hunters communicated through animal calls; assumed characteristics of powerful carnivorous animals; talked of death, blood, and killing; and sang songs of hunting that could not be used around the home. At the end of the hunt or war party, "everything pertaining to killing was put away, everything was pleasant again, and Blessingway songs could be sung" following a purification ritual.[6]

But even the products of the hunt must be used carefully. The horns and bones of a deer were not brought across the San Juan because the sheep would become wild. Another explanation is that the horns were left there to grow into more deer. Fur from tanned deer hides was kept away from livestock; yet if a sheep became sick, it was given the smoke from burned deer hair to keep disease out of the herd. The meat of wild game was never mixed with that of sheep and goats.[7] Thus the peacefulness associated with home, family, and domesticity was not joined with danger, killing, and enemies that lived beyond the boundaries of safety.

Another important body of water in this region is Mancos Creek. Known as Slim-Water Canyon (To Nts'osikooh), this river figures heavily in the stories of Monster Slayer and Born for Water as well as the teachings of the Female Mountainway.[8] The junction of the San Juan and Mancos is particularly powerful, Washington Matthews suggesting that this could be the place where the Diné went to pray for success in war. Sometimes they saw the Twins' forms reflected in the water.

This area is still used for protection ceremonies by medicine men. One person told of his father going to this place to leave offerings and prayers to protect his son, who was in combat in Vietnam. Just as Born for Water waited at this site and prayed while Monster Slayer went to Shiprock to fight two giant birds that were killing the people, so did this father perform the same ceremonies as the hero twin. The prayers and offerings were so powerful a protection for the son in Vietnam that, if some evil were about to destroy him, the father would have received the harm and died instead. Because Mancos Creek is so important in Navajo mythology, the powers have remained there to help the earth-surface people.[9]

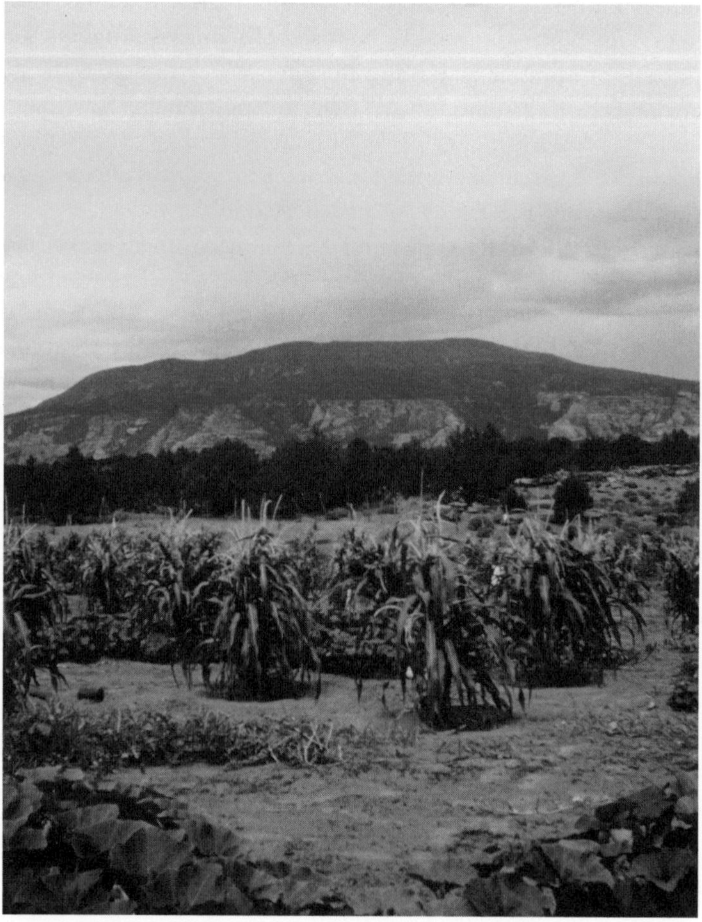

Corn was life to the Navajo. First Man and First Woman were formed from a perfect ear of white corn and yellow corn respectively. This cornfield at Navajo Mountain illustrates the technique of planting common in the Southwest—a marked depression to catch the slightest rainfall and corn grouped in clusters so that the outer stalks protect the inner ones from desert winds and blowing sand.
(Photo by author)

CHAPTER FIVE

Plants

The Bears Ears, Blue Mountain, and Navajo Mountain, as well as the canyons and deserts of the Four Corners region, are important for yet another reason: the gathering and use of plants. The Diné have an extensive knowledge of and appreciation for plants in their many varieties and forms. Vegetation is an important element in life that comes under the control of the holy beings, who in turn work for the benefit of man and animals through the plant people. George Blueeyes, a medicine man, explains:

> The Plant People were put here for us. The sky is the one who does the planting. He moves clouds over the plants. He moves clouds of male rain. He moves the female rain and dark mists over the plants, and they grow. We live by the plants. They are our food and our medicine and the medicine for our livestock. . . . There were more plants long ago. It seemed as if there was no bare ground. Sunflowers covered the earth with yellow, and among them were flowers of red and blue. There were so many different plants. But the plant people move wherever they please. If they choose to go back to the land, they will. You cannot plant these kinds of plants. If they choose to move somewhere else, it is up to them.[1]

The old adage "you are what you eat" is another belief accepted by the Diné. What a biologist calls the web of life is well established in Navajo philosophy, which teaches that man is a part of a natural, cyclical scheme. Harmony comes from understanding this established order. One man explained:

> I learn from observing my surroundings. When I see things work in a certain way, then that is the way it is working. As you can see, we are the plants that live around us. A person grows up on plant juice. Livestock eat certain plants and it makes their meat taste good. A person grows up on this livestock. I do not know how you grow inside the womb, but we grow there and develop. Between man and woman, their juice comes together

> and a baby starts to grow. That is where the holy beings help. Then we become a holy being when we start to move around. So the boys and girls were once part of a plant in some way. When a person tends the sheep, the sheep will eat, eat, eat, and eat. It will be fat. . . . From the sheep, life renews itself. . . . [And so] on the tip of these plants there are horses, cattle, and sheep.[2]

As with most things in the Navajo universe, plants are divided into males and females. The qualities that separate the sexes are sometimes unclear, ranging from descriptions of bark to size, shape, and leaf type. For example, mountain mahogany is used for a male sacrificial cigarette and cliffrose for a female because the male plant is larger and coarser. The bark of a cedar tree is shaggy and thus male; but another version claims that round trees are female and tall ones male. Juniper and pine trees with sharp leaves are male, while a female's are more rounded. Cottonwood trees with "beaded earrings," or seeds, are female; those without are male.[3]

One plant, however, that is clearly defined according to sex is corn. White corn and its pollen are male; yellow corn and pollen are female. In a ceremony this distinction is reinforced, requiring white corn to be placed to the east and yellow to the west, while men use white ground corn to powder their bodies and women use yellow. Because corn is one of the most powerful plants of the Diné, its pollen is extensively used in ceremonies and prayers.[4]

The planting, care, and harvesting of corn in traditional culture was surrounded by religious proscription. Field selection and preparation as well as planting involved both ritual and hard work. Certain taboos also entered in. During the planting, pregnant women could not help because the corn would not be healthy. It might shrivel and die, act like jealous children, or become deformed. A menstruating woman prevented seeds from growing and caused the soil to turn red. A game of shinny played in a cornfield brought rodents and sandstorms. When wind started to damage crops, medicine men used a ceremonial name to talk to the wind, telling it to leave the plants alone. Songs were used to warn lightning away, the singer requesting that it remain high and not strike the earth.[5]

Knowledge of wild plants is passed on from one generation to the next, from grandmother to mother or daughter and from father to son. This is specialized knowledge that requires identifying the plants and understanding the proper way to pick or dig them. One person suggested that female plants or parts of plants needed to come from female mountains, like Black Mesa, and male plants and parts from male mountains, like the Chuskas.[6] Others indicated no knowledge of this but asserted that it was the type of plant—male or female—that mattered.

A wide area may be traveled to get the right type of vegetation. A medicine woman from Aneth told of going to Blue Mountain, Mesa Verde, Ute Mountain, the Carrizo Mountains, Navajo Mountain, and the La Sals—an area with a diameter of about one hundred and fifty miles. Within these boundaries there were sacred places where gifts were given in thanks to the earth for providing the plants that she took. She left corn pollen, turquoise, white shell, and prayers at sites on the eastern tip of Little Cahone Mesa, at lightning-struck junipers, and on top of Cahone Mesa.[7]

More common is the process of leaving an offering at a plant that represents the ones to be picked. Mary Blueeyes tells of the procedure she goes through:

> When you are making herbs for a woman, the plant is given a white shell [if for a man—turquoise], then particles of ntł'iz, and then corn pollen. As you are praying to these plants, you tell them who you are taking the plants to. You say that you are going to put this on Naatii Dezbaa', even though the person may not go by that name. You tell the plant what area of the person's body needs to be healed, then the reason you came to get it. The plants are tended by the holy people who give the plants rain. This is the reason for the prayer. Then you thank the holy people for the plant, request them to heal where the pain is, and ask for the well-being of the person you are treating with this medicine.[8]

The sacred name of the plant is used. The power from the plant heals the person by supernatural aid, but the medicine man or woman who picked it becomes the shield between the sick person and the illness. Just knowing about a certain flower or root is not enough to heal; it is the origin of its use, the prayers that accompany it, and the way it is gathered that form the contract between the holy being and the patient.[9] The plant that is given the offering is not the one that is picked but one that is left to give the message to the supernaturals. If those that are harvested are in a group, they are taken out in order, starting with those furthest east, then those furthest west, then those furthest south, and finally those furthest north, reinforcing the pattern of male and female.[10]

Navajo use of plants is a mixture of religious mythology and home remedy. Myths and stories may describe both the illness and the cure, which is often based on the principle of what anthropologists call sympa-

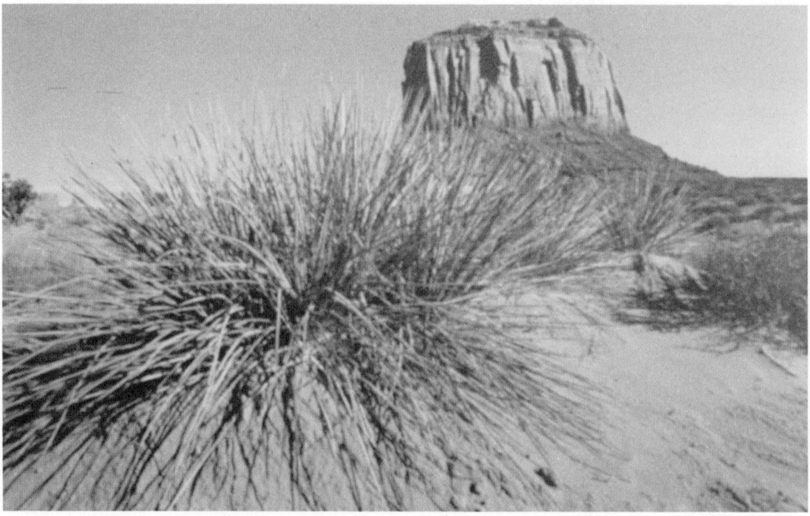

Yucca in Navajo mythology was a plant that gave men and women their feelings towards each other. The holy beings took yucca, yucca fruit, and sacred waters and rubbed them over the man and woman's heart so that they would love each other. Yet as with most things in the Navajo world, there was also a negative side—in this instance, the start of jealousy. *(Photo by Stan Byrd)*

Many of the trees found on Blue Mountain and elsewhere have specific uses and teachings about them. Oak, for instance, provides wood to make the traditional bow and arrow, the bow for the cradleboard, and a medicine to soften afterbirth pains. Rotted pine is used as talcum powder, while the inner bark of ponderosa pine can be eaten. *(Photo by Tom Austin)*

thetic magic, or "like begets like." For instance, red Indian paintbrush is put in water and given to stop a nosebleed. If it fails to stop, a person sprinkles powdered mountain sheep horn onto the coals of a fire and the afflicted person puts his head in the smoke. One is not supposed to blow into bottle plant because it will bother his bladder, but the plant is used for someone who has presumably urinated on an ant and now has trouble with elimination. The gray dust from aspen bark is put on a girl's face during the kinaaldá ceremony, so that, like the bark, her skin will stay smooth and free from wrinkles and so that, like the tree, she will remain straight and will not become bent with age.[11]

In caring for their livestock the Diné use plants to heal and protect. For instance, snakeweed is pounded with a stone, put in water, and given to sheep and calves orally as well as in a poultice for a cut. When sheep get an eye disease, the stem that protrudes out of a yucca plant is burned, the ashes are crushed and mixed with salt, and the ingredients are put on the infected eye. Larkspur may be eaten by both goats and women to make them prolific.

The shredded bark of cliffrose is used for diapers. It also serves to calm sheep that have grazed over deer hair and bones, since merely being in the proximity of undomesticated animals causes them to act wild and run away from their owner. Along with cliffrose, devil's claw, silky sophora, and plants that the deer have rubbed their antlers on are collected and mixed, then put on the sheep to keep them calm. This medicine is also used for people who have been carrying a deer or tanning its hide and have become sickened from this contact. If young men and women are unmanageable, this potion also quiets them.

Narrowleaf yucca root is crushed and used for shampoo. Its tender stalks can be placed under a fire; when cooked, they taste like corn. If the stalks are fried, they taste like squash. Broadleaf yucca is a remedy for vomiting and heartburn. People soak their feet in crushed sunflowers and water to remove the odor. Mint is used to remove children's fever. It is placed in cool water and then given to the child orally, after which the entire body is washed. Mint, along with rock lichens, is used to cure mouth sores.

Coniferous trees are also important. The cones from ponderosa pines are burned and the ashes placed on sores. The pitch from this tree is mixed with grease and put on infected sores or chapped skin. When given on a spoon, this concoction helps fight pneumonia and whooping cough as it opens the breathing passage. For those who want long hair, ponderosa pine needles soaked in water help its growth. The gum from the piñon tree is medicine that is good for a woman who injures her breast. It can also be used on a sheep that breaks its leg. The injured part is treated with the medicine and then wrapped in cloth.

Ailments connected with birth are also healed with plants. Spreading fleabane is crushed and added to water, then given to a pregnant woman. This is to prevent the umbilical cord from wrapping around the baby and strangling it during childbirth. The malady is caused by a person lassoing a horse or another animal in the unborn baby's presence. If a woman has intercourse directly after giving birth, she may be afflicted with internal sores. The cure for this is to find a juniper and a piñon tree growing out of the same spot. They are given ntł'iz and prayers, after which a medicinal drink is made of juniper, piñon, scrub oak, oak, sumac, and mountain mahogany.

There are also plants that are said to be able to change the sex of a baby before it is born. A pregnant woman can ingest parry bellflower and receive a female baby. The same effects are obtained by taking a white cowry shell that is folded inward on both sides, grinding it into powder, and then eating it. For a boy, the same thing is done with turquoise. Few-flowered goldenrod is made into a lotion to bathe a hermaphrodite when it is born to make the child sensible.

Mormon tea mixed with snakeweed can cure diarrhea. After Mormon tea receives corn pollen, the stems that protrude from the bush are picked and brewed to make a tea. For those who are balding and would like to get some hair back, there is a small plant that grows in the cracks of rocks where water seeps out. This plant and another that looks like rabbitbrush are boiled, making a shampoo. For those not lucky enough to find the right plants, the first urine from a firstborn baby also keeps the hair from falling out.

Plants also provide protection from natural elements. Leaves of creeping barberry that happen to point north and flowers or berries of that plant positioned to the west are picked and sprinkled on lightning-struck grass near livestock. Alumroot is smoked in a jet pipe by a person whose body has become twisted by a whirlwind moving in a counterclockwise (evil) direction. Protection from snakes and lightning comes from *Tragia neptaefolia,* the former being repelled by a lotion made from the plant and the latter by sprinkling the leaves around the hogan. If a person kills a green-collared lizard by accident, death is prevented by drinking or eating the steeped roots of goldenrod within four days of the incident.[12]

This brief explanation of a few of the plants the Diné use illustrates how important the vegetation of the mountains and deserts is. One man explained the close relationship of earth, plants, and animals this way:

> The earth is our mother. The sky is our father. Just as a man gives his wife beautiful things to wear, so our Father Sky does the same. He sends rain down on Mother Earth, and because of the rain the plants grow, and flowers of many different colors appear. She in turn provides food for him. He dresses her as a man would dress his woman. He moves clouds of male rain. He moves dark mists and female rain. Dark mists cloak the ground, and plants grow with many colored blossoms. The plants with colored blossoms are her dress. It wears out. Yes, the earth's cover wears out. The plants ripen and fade away in the fall. Then in the spring when the rains come again, Mother Earth once again puts on her finery. The plants are restored again in beauty. This is what the stories of the elders say.[13]

To Navajos, animals serve as patterns for life, models of social interaction, icons with power, and metaphors of destruction. Deer, in addition to providing hides used for clothing and medicine bundles, supply meat that is said to be medicine because the herbs they eat are the same ones used in ceremonies. (Photo by Jeffrey Thomson)

CHAPTER SIX

Animals

The Navajo people are quick to point out their dependence on the land for plants and water. Of equal importance are the animals. Classifying them into two groups, domestic and wild, the Diné have a complex set of rituals and beliefs that stress man's relationship to animals. Because this knowledge ranges over a vast array from insects to reptiles to mammals, only a sampling can be given here, with an emphasis on some of the more important creatures.

Interestingly, perhaps the most influential animal to affect the life of the Diné was not native to the American Southwest but was introduced by the Spanish. Soon after their arrival, sheep became a major economic, social, and religious consideration in traditional Navajo life. People measured their status in society, the welfare of their family, and their blessings from the holy beings by taking stock of their herds. Food, blankets, clothing, and money came from them. The following story illustrates how closely entwined this animal was in the Navajo economy. One day, a sheep in poor condition came upon a bee'adizí (a tool to twist wool). The tool thought of how ugly the bedraggled sheep looked, with its wool coming off and its skinny body peeking through, and so told the animal that it was unpleasant to look at. The sheep agreed but returned later, fully clothed in wool, to display itself to the bee'adizí, and the two agreed that they were now both beautiful. They shook hands and are today inseparable. The sheep and the bee'adizí need each other.[1]

Dogs are another part of the sheepherding economy. One person explained that dogs make money for the Diné and make their economy work because they chase the coyotes away. The dogs do not get to eat the mutton they deserve, but they must be treated nicely because they know part of the Enemyway ceremony. If a person beats a dog, it may sing part of this song and kill the miscreant. Dogs also hold special powers against skinwalkers, because canines are not affected by witchcraft. For this same reason, a medicine man practicing witchcraft could not keep a dog, since the animal would know what the man was like and would not stay. It also has the ability to bring about poverty, as do horses and sheep. Because they understand the voice of man, when a person curses these animals it is like cursing another human.[2]

Domestic animals are gifts to the people. Owners say figuratively that they contain wealth such as money, gold, jewelry, and other goods. The story of the burro is a good example, illustrating the importance of livestock in the Navajo economy. First Man formed many different kinds of animals out of precious jewels such as white shell, turquoise, abalone, and jet. When he was through, he had a large pile of refuse which some children found and decided to play in. They created from this scrap an animal with hooves made of jet, a nose of ash, a body of refuse, legs striped with coal, ears of a jackrabbit, cattail fuzz for hair, and a tail of worm material, after which they sprinkled the being with star dust. The burro's internal organs were another concern. They fashioned its heart and lungs from red stone, liver from turquoise, intestines from white shell, and a tongue from a combination of leftovers. Wind blew breath into the creature so that it would live. Its braying sounded funny because its mouth was made of scraps. The children laughed at the funny sight and mocked the animal, but Black God cautioned them not to look at its outside but what was inside. And so it is with people. One should look at the heart and not the outward appearance or else he poisons himself.[3]

In Navajo mythology, animals are really humans with a different outer form. Often they will go into a mountain, cave, or hill and take off this physical exterior and act like people. They have sacred powers and knowledge that can be used when proper respect is shown.

Although animals, insects, and birds were with the Diné as they emerged from the underworlds, they received many of their qualities in this world. There are stories that tell why animals have certain characteristics and powers. One story which should delight any reader concerns a shoe game that brought all of the creatures together to decide if a day should be all light or dark. Because this game is played only at night, the night creatures met the day creatures at sunset and started the competition. They hid a colored yucca ball beneath the shoes and passed it back and forth between team members. Gopher burrowed underground and came up under the shoes to see where the ball was hidden but found that it was not under any of them. To this day, however, when a person gets a hole in the sole of his shoe it is because of Gopher. Owl was hiding the ball in his claws. Squirrel, a member of the other team, took a stick and hit Owl, knocking the ball loose, flattening the bird's beak, and causing its claws to assume a clutching position. Coyote, true to his devious self, ran from side to side, depending on which group was leading at the time. Some cried and some sang as the game roared on through the night.

The creatures, except for Owl, did not notice that the sun was rising in the east, but he had the ball and did not want to stop. Finally the game ended and the stakes — beautiful colored rocks and sand — were hurriedly divided. Some of the creatures were fortunate, like Bluebird, who got turquoise for a color. Prairie Dog took sand. Skunk got ashes, as did Crow, but one of the animals wanted to make Skunk different and so took some white paint and ran it down his back. The animals joked and made fun of each other's colors, with Buzzard pouring red sand on his head. Snake wriggled through his materials and that is why he has a pattern. Coyote, who made the rules of the shoe game, got gray for his coat but was not satisfied and so added off-white. Horned Toad, a day creature, sang the songs for the game and picked out the colors that would help him hide. Eagle took all of the pretty colors left over and mixed them through his feathers.

The animals rushed back to their homes so as not to be caught by the sun. Mountain Lion had his fur tinted by sunlight, his black mouth being the only part of him that shows his connection to night. Bear also had his back tinted by the red light of dawn as he lumbered back to the mountains. He was in such a hurry that he put his shoes on the wrong feet, and that is the way they are now. Since no one group won the game, today there is an equal amount of day and night.[4]

The Diné observe animal characteristics very closely. The qualities they ascribe to them are important in their views of how the natural world operates. For instance, rats and mice are a bad sign because they live in graves and feed on the dead, so the Diné burn things eaten by them. Chipmunks, on the other hand, are good friends and guides, have knowledge of how to kill monsters, and can determine if a monster is actually dead or just pretending. Their strong power is one reason why medicine pouches are often made from their skins. They are also said to be a very "American" animal because they are colored red, white, and blue. Squirrels are quick-footed thieves. The Diné hang a squirrel tail from a cradleboard to make the baby nimble and sure-footed. Porcupines, or "many-needles," have a variety of uses. Besides eating the meat, the Diné burn quills as an inhalant for congestion and use the ashes for healing sores. Skunks also have healing powers. Tails and skins are hung in a hogan and the meat is eaten to help cure tuberculosis. Their musk is an inhalant for colds and a treatment for mouth sores.

It is also said that Skunk joined with Coyote in the origination of cheating and dishonesty when they worked together to trick other animals out of their possessions.[5] The story starts with Coyote, whose fur is dressed in rain. The dark rain clouds are on his body, as is the yellow light of breaking day and evening twilight. One day he called the clouds on top of him and asked for a sprinkle of rain. He asked for water to squish between his toes, then raised the level to his knees, then his back, then his ears, and finally requested enough to float on to a place where there were many prairie dogs. His wish was granted.

He eventually climbed onto dry land and was lying in the sun when Skunk came to the river to get water. Coyote gained his attention and hatched a plan whereby Skunk would lure the prairie dogs to Coyote's supposedly dead body, and together the two would club them to death. The plan worked, Skunk spraying his mist into the air and helping Coyote to kill the animals.

Coyote, being greedy, asked Skunk if he would agree to a race, winner take all. Skunk thought this a good idea; and so, after they put the supper in the fire, the race began. Skunk, however, just went over a rise, waited in a badger hole for Coyote to pass, then went back to the fire, took the supper to a rock ledge, and ate. Coyote returned later, discarded the four small prairie dogs left in the fire, and pleaded for some of the good meat. Skunk showed no mercy, so Coyote had no choice but to go on to other adventures, having learned an important lesson about trickery.[6]

Coyote has, in fact, become the symbol of this and other antisocial qualities. Known as First Scolder, First One to Use Force, and Fine Young Chief Howling in the Dawn beyond the East, he is shrewd, mischievous, undependable, licentious, foolish, and persistent. His penchant for not following directions and being disobedient in sacred matters leads to a series of mishaps. His trials with Changing Bear Maiden, his scattering of the stars, and his choice of October as his month because it is "mixed up" or changing are just a few examples of how his thinking affects mankind. He brought death into the world by saying that if a stone he tossed into the water floated to the surface there would be no death. But stones do not float and so man does not live forever. Though he cannot be killed because his life force is in his tail and nose, others must die. Just his presence may ruin a person's day; and so pollen or turquoise is put on his tracks by anyone who crosses his path. Many principles, however, in

Navajo culture are taught by viewing the results of his antisocial behavior. His failure to live by proper standards serves as a lesson to mortals that there is a right way to live and consequences accompany those acts that are not in harmony with correct principles.[7]

Other powerful creatures in the Navajo universe are bears. Often considered to be as much human as animal, they are shown the respect owed to holy beings. Bears are creatures that can heal and help and are not to be ridiculed. They live in the mountains and so figure heavily in the Mountain Chant as protectors whose powers are so strong that even their tracks are treated with respect. The Diné believe that the holy beings assigned bears to live in the Chuska-Tunicha range and never to cross over to Black Mesa. To permit them to do so would bring bad luck, so the Diné direct efforts to keep bears out of the Chinle Valley that lies between the two mountain ranges.[8]

Because bears are so much like humans, they are talked to and reasoned with. The killing of a bear, though done only under certain circumstances, was usually accompanied by prayers and an explanation. If it was to be killed during a time of starvation, the hunter stood outside its den and said, "Though you are eaten, you will return whole to your own people and will become chief over your own people." The leader then sang a song to lure it out of the den and addressed it by its sacred name, The Fine Young Chief Roaming in the Woods.[9] Medicine men also sang songs to avoid contact with bears. First the male bear and then the female was called and told that they could not be seen and then were warned not to steal.

Navajo Oshley told of such an experience with bears. He spent two months herding sheep on Dibé Ntsaa in an area that had ripening berries and many bear tracks. He explained:

> In the night, the bears came to eat the berries and I could hear the snapping of branches, so I went out and told the bear not to eat on this side [of the mountain] because there were sheep nearby. For the rest of the night, they stayed on their side to eat the berries. The bear listened if it was talked to.... I butchered a sheep that was nice and fat. I packed the meat away and hung it up in a tree. I went after the sheep to gather them in one place and when I came back to my camp, the meat was gone. I thought maybe the supply man came and got the meat, but there were no such tracks. The only tracks were from a bear. The sack for the meat was untied and not even ripped but just left on the ground. I wondered how the bear could do such a neat job of untying the meat. I butchered another fat sheep late in

The bear is one of the most powerful creatures in Navajo mythology. As First Man named some of the animals, Bear protested the name he received. The holy being said "shash" to quiet him; Bear repeated it four times, felt it had a strange sound and awesome feeling, and so decided to keep the name. *(Photo by Calvin Black)*

> the afternoon. It was then time to check on the sheep again. As I hung up the meat, I said that whoever took the meat ought to try to get this off. . . . I got back to the campsite and the meat was gone again. Only the rope was on the ground. I thought that the supply man had come and gotten the meat. The only tracks there were bear tracks and the rope was again untied. I went to where the sack was and there were no bite marks. I began to realize they were like human beings. Two days later I told the bears not to eat on this side and they listened to what I said to them. . . .
>
> Bears do not frighten me. I just tell the bear to leave me alone, and they do not bother me. My maternal grandmother told me that if a bear should block my way, and it does not move from that place, I should take my shoes off and throw them to the bear and that would get the bear to move out of my way. A couple of days later, this happened. I asked a bear as I took off my shoe what he was doing in my path. Then I told him that here was my shoe and the bear took off into the bushes. . . . If I had not done that I do not know what would have happened. This was the rule that a bear would obey.
>
> About two days later, I had a rifle with me and I saw the bear where I usually hung my food up. I shot at it but missed and then it growled at me. I was still quite a distance from the campsite where I cooked my supper. I thought about what happened that day, then went to sleep. In my dream I thought a man came to me. He was really tall, had a bushy mustache, and asked why I was shooting at him, so I told him he had brought it on himself. The person walked off without saying anything. . . . The white man told me to kill the bears and I said no. I remember what my grandmother and my elders told me and that was why I did not kill the bears. The next morning I offered the bear corn pollen. I called him grandfather and told him I was thankful that he was talking nicely with me. I told him from then on I would not do it again. I had already said I would not harm them and I kept my word.[10]

Deer are also animals that must be treated and hunted with respect. Like all creatures, they are under the control of Talking God and Black God, who release them for man's use. In the past, before the men went hunting, they took a sweat bath during which they sang songs encouraging these gods to give them the best meat. Talking God and Black God taught these songs, saying, "We will not hide the deer from you, for they are your livestock, your food. We will place them in front of you, but you must keep these songs sacred. From the time you leave the sweathouse until the time you come home, keep to the holy way."[11]

In order for a hunter to maintain sacred thoughts, he avoided pointing a finger and saying "far away" because the game might hear and avoid the hunter; he could not shoot at crows, wolves, or coyotes because they helped to locate game, just as a screech owl's call at night indicated the direction to hunt. The men attempted to act and think like animals and used animal voices to communicate with each other. When a deer died, the hunter turned its head toward camp so that the minds of other animals would also go in that direction, while the men were careful not to breathe a dying deer's breath because it might make them sick.

Deer entrails and horns were treated in a ceremonially prescribed manner to please the gods and to insure that new deer could grow from the remains. Failure to show proper respect affected not only how many deer were available for future hunts but also the amount of rain, because these animals were in close contact with the holy beings who controlled rain.[12] Since they lived in the mountains, they were protected by thunder and lightning; their antlers were not brought home because they attracted electrical storms; and because deer fed on sacred, medicinal plants, to eat their meat was to ingest medicine. Buckskin still serves as a shield of protection, and medicine men make certain sacred pouches from deer hide.

Like the deer, mountain sheep live in the mountains and are protected by lightning and thunder. Called Walk in Thunder, they are said to be immune to the effects of lightning, have strong supernatural powers, and create thunder when rams butt heads. Although the meat is not eaten, the hide is used to make medicine bags, which can protect a home from lightning. The skin between the horns on the forehead is massaged on aching muscles to relieve pain, while the fat is mixed with red and black pigments to drive evil away from a sick person.[13]

Other creatures also have powers. Snakes are involved in bringing rain because they move like lightning, while the drops of water coming down in sheets appear as male and female snakes. Molest a snake and the rains will stop. Horned toads make the arrowheads found lying on the ground by blowing on a rock and chipping its sides. The power of a dragonfly can be obtained by sprinkling corn pollen on one and then putting the pollen in a horse's mouth to help it run faster. Butterflies, on the other hand, are a symbol of temptation and foolishness, and, along with moths, they symbolize the insanity that comes from breaking taboos like incest.[14]

Each animal, bird, or insect, therefore, has its place in the animate Navajo universe. Each in its own way illustrates or provides the necessary power of protection for a harmonious life—or is the harbinger of punishment for violations of taboos.

The entire world is a storehouse of teachings that help a person to understand the realities of life. They are not children's fairy tales to be laughed at but are a way of looking at a living world. Everything has a spirit, is male or female, controls power, teaches a lesson, deserves respect, and has its place. This power is reached through ceremony, song, and prayer and provides protection in a world filled with the vagaries of life. But it is the life of the Diné, and it is one of beauty.

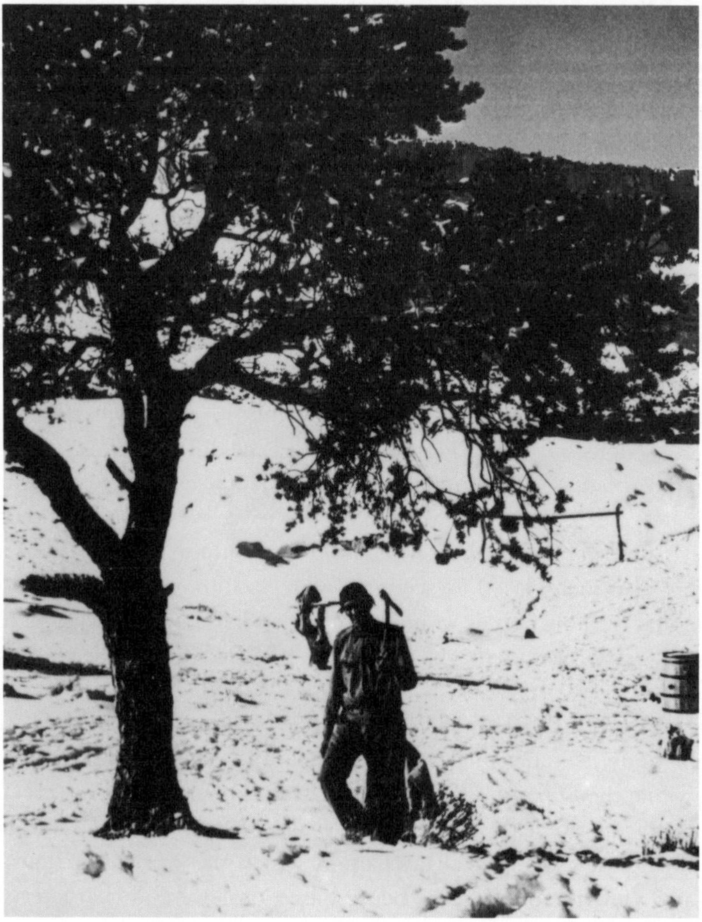

Old Man Jack. Navajos believe there are several different types of snow and name each according to its peculiar quality. "On the branch snow" sticks only to tree branches, fences, and wires and melts in a few hours; "horse tracks snow" is so thin that a horse's hoofs expose the bare ground; and an "in-law chaser" is a big snowstorm with heavy dark clouds. Supposedly the son-in-law must hustle about, chopping wood, hauling water, and doing chores before the blizzard strikes.
(Photo courtesy Harold B. Lee Library)

CHAPTER SEVEN

Sacredness of the Physical World

What, then, is one to think of this spiritual power that pervades the physical world? Such anthropological terms as animism, animatism, and anthropopsychism must extend far beyond book definitions to attain the feelings that older Navajos have toward the land. Indeed, for some, this whole topic becomes one of life and death. While conducting interviews about sacred geography with an older woman, I asked what seemed a fairly innocuous question: "How can one tell the difference between male and female plants?" She emphatically replied that to divulge such information was not possible because this knowledge was what was keeping her alive. One person in Bluff, when talking about the Navajo Twins, told her story and then closed by saying, "Now you know my secret." Many believe that the holy beings would be offended if too much was said, if the place was inappropriate for the transfer of knowledge, or if the season was incorrect.

The basis of this thinking lies in how one perceives the world. Western thought finds its roots in the Renaissance and, later, in the Enlightenment, while the Diné find theirs in a mythic explanation of the creation. Francis Bacon, René Descartes, and Isaac Newton helped establish a mechanistic view of natural laws upon which the world functions; the Diné also view the universe as being based on laws and characteristics, but they have different underlying assumptions. The former stresses the physical nature and structure of objects that can be manipulated through mechanical means, while the latter emphasizes the supernatural or spiritual side of an object and uses its animate powers to obtain aid.

Both views categorize according to their underlying assumptions. For the Diné, everything in the universe is either male or female, so that the qualities exhibited by humans are transferred to both animate and inanimate things. The male is rough, strong, violent, and destructive; the female is gentle, weak, and nurturing.

The distinction between living and nonliving entities is also different in Navajo culture, because everything is alive, has power, and needs respect. This point was dramatically driven home one time when I was interviewing a medicine woman. I asked her to tell me the story about the Bears Ears, but she said it was the wrong place and time of year and that the winter was the correct time. Later that day we were on Blue Mountain collecting herbs and so I asked again. She consented, saying that the mountain would be there to witness and so it was all right. When she was through, we continued collecting plants, and within an hour's time we had worked our way to a reservoir at the foot of the mountain. Dark, male storm clouds gathered, the wind increased, and jagged bolts of lightning creased the skies. By the time we returned to the truck, rain was splashing over the countryside in a typical late-afternoon midsummer thundershower.

To an Anglo observer, the reason for this phenomenon included orographic storms, convection currents, and cloud saturation. The real reason to the Navajo participants was that the holy beings were pleased by the telling of the story and so sent the rain as a statement. Both explanations are, according to a dictionary definition, rational, "having or exercising the ability to reason . . . and be logical."[1] The world view of the Anglo forces the issue to be addressed in physical terms that are empirical. The Diné feel more comfortable in explaining the same phenomenon through supernatural means.

This is not to suggest that parts of these elements do not exist in the other's view, because they do; but they are not central to core beliefs used to explain the world. For instance, the Diné understand that there are plants that heal people and animals. The curative powers are linked to a story, ceremony, or the plant's appearance, instead of its chemical properties. Conversely, a scientist will throw his hands in the air when asked how prayer works. If he acknowledges that prayer is answered, his explanation will probably follow along the lines of faith healing, psychological comfort, or luck, since the same result may not be achieved every time the "experiment" is conducted. The Diné, on the other hand, feel comfortable operating in this realm.

The basis for understanding the world is supplied through stories—myths, legends, and tales—that explain how and why things function as they do. The stories can be as serious as the Twins killing the monsters to make life safe for the earth-surface people or as light as Coyote's being disconsolate, scuffing his feet, and removing a rock from a ledge. The knowledge shared in these stories is the basis for ceremonies and the rules for daily behavior. They encapsulate Navajo views and explanations of life and hold as much truth and power as any book on atomic theory or plate tectonics. Leslie Marmon Silko, a Laguna author, said of the oral tradition, "I will tell you something about stories; they aren't just entertainment. Don't be fooled. They are all we have, you see, all we have to fight off illness and death. You don't have anything if you don't have the stories."[2]

So it is with the Diné. The stories, tied to the land in rock formations, rivers, plants, and animals, give proof of religious validity. Just as stained glass windows of the cathedrals built in the Middle Ages served the illiterate as a picture book of the tenets of Christianity, so do landforms for the Diné. The land serves as a mnemonic device that jogs the memory into remembering events and lessons associated with it. Mircea Eliade calls it a hierophany or an event associated with a place where "something sacred shows itself."[3]

Just as another religion might insist that reading the scriptures, going to a church or temple, or meditating in a certain place increases the chances of inspiration or supernatural aid, so does the land serve a similar purpose for the Navajo people. The Holy Land in the Middle East, with its Jerusalem, Garden of Gethsemane, and Golgotha, are of no greater import to Christians than the Diné's holy land is to them, circumscribed as it is by sacred mountains and containing the junction of the San Juan River and Mancos Creek, where Born for Water invoked supernatural aid to overcome danger and death, and the Bears Ears, where good triumphed over evil.

The power that originally helped those in need is still there, residing in the holy beings. When a prayer is given, ntł'iz offered, and a proper attitude exhibited, this power is manifested. The sacred forces are responsive to correct intent and procedure; but as with anything that holds power, discretion is important. Electricity provides a good analogy. When used properly, it powers lights, heats stoves, runs machinery, and protects people from harm. If improper conductors are used, or incorrect voltage is applied, the abusers are shocked or destroyed. To the Diné, improper use of supernatural power may result in both physical and spiritual harm, since the two are inseparable.

Good and evil are also inseparable. A site or prayer that is used for positive effect can also be used for negative results by just reversing that which is good. Places for witchcraft can be cleansed and used for good, just as prayers for the Blessingway, if said in reverse, can bring evil. By

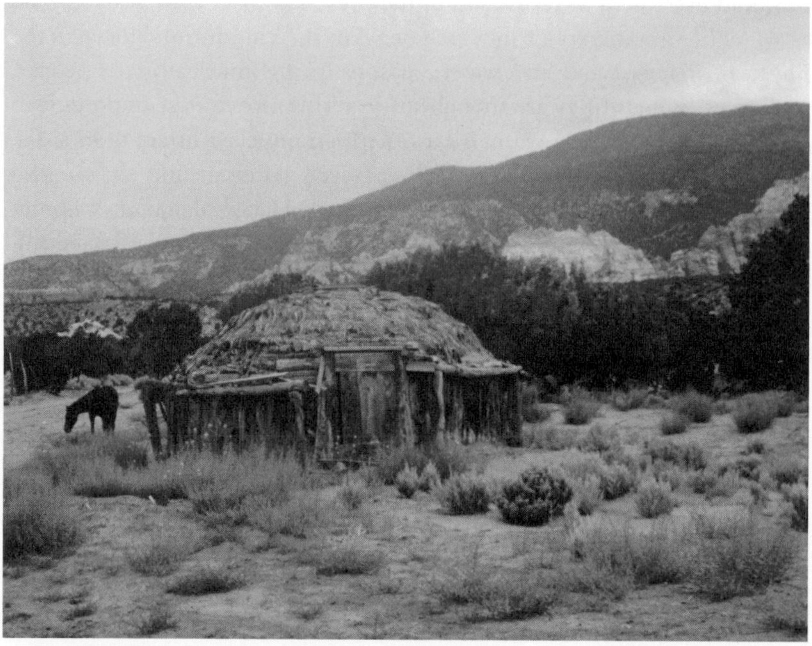

Many older Navajos still keep in their hogan a "mountain soil bundle" that contains earth from the sacred mountains and things from other holy places. As John Holiday, a medicine man from Monument Valley, explained, "These bundles hold wisdom, sound language, sacred songs, and prayers—everything that makes up your life. It is to keep things in order, at peace, and prosperous." *(Photo by author)*

going to the place where the mythic event occurred, one participates in a recreation of the past and draws those powers to one's aid. The previous examples of the soldier who was protected by prayers said at certain places, the medicine man who collected earth from the sacred mountains, and the prayers offered before crossing the San Juan River all illustrate this principle. Thus a person participates with powers exhibited in the past and uses them to secure aid in the present.

All of life is a metaphor in which one reenacts the spiritual through the physical. Places, wind and water, seasons and climate, objects, people, and other living things are thought of in terms of qualities important to Navajo values. Once, a woman sat quietly in my class listening to a discussion in which she was emotionally involved. After a while, she erupted in a display of anger that she later regretted. Her explanation was that when she was a little girl a medicine man had blessed her with bear medicine, which imbedded these qualities in her personality.

The land and its creatures also help interpret what is happening in general. As sacred sites become profaned by people who are ignorant or forgetful of ceremonial observances, the holy beings depart. The bonds with a living myth are broken. Some old people feel that the younger generation is the cause of many problems the Diné face today. The youth do not place corn pollen in the rivers, so now the waters are polluted and destroy the people. Prayers are no longer learned to approach a sacred area, and so people have fear of certain places. Additionally, outsiders have profaned the land. Because the Diné no longer have access to parts of the Navajo-Hopi Joint-use Area, their minds are troubled. The Glen Canyon Dam blocks the lifeblood of the earth, causing it to sicken. One woman explained that the 1986 space shuttle disaster was doomed from the outset because of scientists tampering with the affairs of the gods. She said, "These white scientists are always trying to test the powers of the supernatural in space.... They should have realized the wind and rain delaying the takeoff was a sign that this mission was doomed."[4]

For the Diné, the land and its inhabitants form a web of life that is both physical and supernatural. Inextricably bound to the religious beliefs of the Navajo people, the mountains, heavens, earth, rocks, plants, animals, and weather enunciate these values. To disregard them is to ignore the essence of Navajo thought and belief with their accompanying aid from the holy beings. Failure to adhere to these principles leads to the most disastrous of all problems in traditional culture—a failure of power, prayers, and protection.

This Anasazi rock art panel, in Montezuma Canyon, Utah, illustrates Pueblo II or III styles. Some Navajos believe that panels such as this describe problems and trials the Anasazis had before they were destroyed—or before they moved from the area. (Photo by author)

PART TWO

Navajo Perception of the Anasazi: The Past as Prologue

The Four Corners region is covered with thousands of prehistoric sites belonging to the Anasazi. Although these people have been studied extensively by archaeologists, researchers have paid little attention to views held by Native American inhabitants of this locale. The Diné have a particularly rich body of lore that explains the history, culture, and ultimate destruction of these prehistoric people. One quickly learns that the Navajo perception of the Anasazi tells much more about the Diné's views of their own world than it does about these ancient peoples. Thus, the purpose of this section is to investigate the importance of the Anasazi as expressed in Navajo mythology.

Before doing so, however, a few limits need to be established. Anthropologists and archaeologists for some time have suggested that the Anasazi abandonment of the San Juan drainage by approximately A.D. 1300 could have been effected by an influx of less-advanced hunters and gatherers who overpowered them, forcing their departure. Many social scientists argue that the arrival of the Diné in the Southwest corresponds roughly with this chronological time frame of abandonment, while others claim that there is no proof of widespread warfare, that their arrival was actually later, and that climatic, ecological, and social reasons were more likely to have caused the departure.[1] There is no definitive answer to this question, though the search for it leads through a voluminous corpus of articles, reports, and books that reach far beyond the scope of this book. But to summarize the issue, David M. Brugge, a noted ethnohistorian, points out that by 1300 the Navajo and other Athabaskan-speaking peoples must have been close to the periphery of the Anasazi region and that they moved into this area shortly after the prehistoric people departed.[2]

Another topic to be bypassed is the historic influence of Pueblo peoples upon the Diné. The infusion of their culture through trade, intermarriage, and forced relocation after the Pueblo Revolt of 1680 may bear fruitful results for further research. But here, the focus of attention is on the Navajo view of who the Anasazi were and their impact on the Navajo people to this day.

The word Anasazi, more correctly spelled 'anaasází ('anaa'—war, alien, enemy, and sází—ancestor, ancestral) is of Navajo origin and means "ancestral aliens or enemies."[3] While social scientists use this term with a fair amount of precision to denote the prehistoric puebloan cultures living in southwestern Colorado, northwestern New Mexico, southern Utah, and northern Arizona between the birth of Christ and A.D. 1300, the Diné apply it on a somewhat broader scale. To them, the word refers to primarily pueblo-dwelling, pottery-making ancients that encompass not only the Anasazi culture just described but also Sinagua, Hohokam, Mogollon, and other cultures that fit into the broader category.[4] For the purpose of this discussion, recorded incidents and interviews focus on the peoples of the Four Corners region.

The canyons and mesas of the Colorado Plateau are covered with thousands of Anasazi sites, some large and others small. They stand as mute testimony to a numerous population that once used the lands intensively and then departed.

By A.D. 1300 the San Juan drainage was no longer the home of the Anasazi, who, according to most anthropologists, moved south to their present locations along the Rio Grande or into the Zuñi, Acoma, or Hopi villages. These people left behind their homes of mud and stone; trails that crisscrossed the land; pictographs and petroglyphs on rock walls; and artifacts such as pottery, projectile points, medicine bundles, and other objects used in daily life.

Their departure was just the beginning for the Diné, who entered the deserted lands and inhabited a region already rich in heritage. However, the Diné were a cautious people, living in a world populated with animate forces, both natural and supernatural, that needed to be reckoned with in order to maintain harmony. A varied body of lore evolved about who the Anasazi were and why they had departed so rapidly, but an equally important understanding developed about what these people left behind.

Since most things in the Navajo universe have some type of power, it was natural that this belief be extended to ruins and artifacts of the Anasazi. It is therefore appropriate to analyze these beliefs and the seeming dichotomy that entails both the use and avoidance of things connected to these prehistoric people.

One should understand that no culture's views are static. What may have been acceptable or unacceptable in the past may be highly desirable or undesirable in the present. Little attempt is made here to chart shifts in attitude or to document causal factors, though some cases are more easily explained than others. Instead, the main focus is on showing that the remnants of Anasazi culture play an important part in Navajo life and that anthropologists and archaeologists need to be alert to the use of these remains in relation to Navajo beliefs.

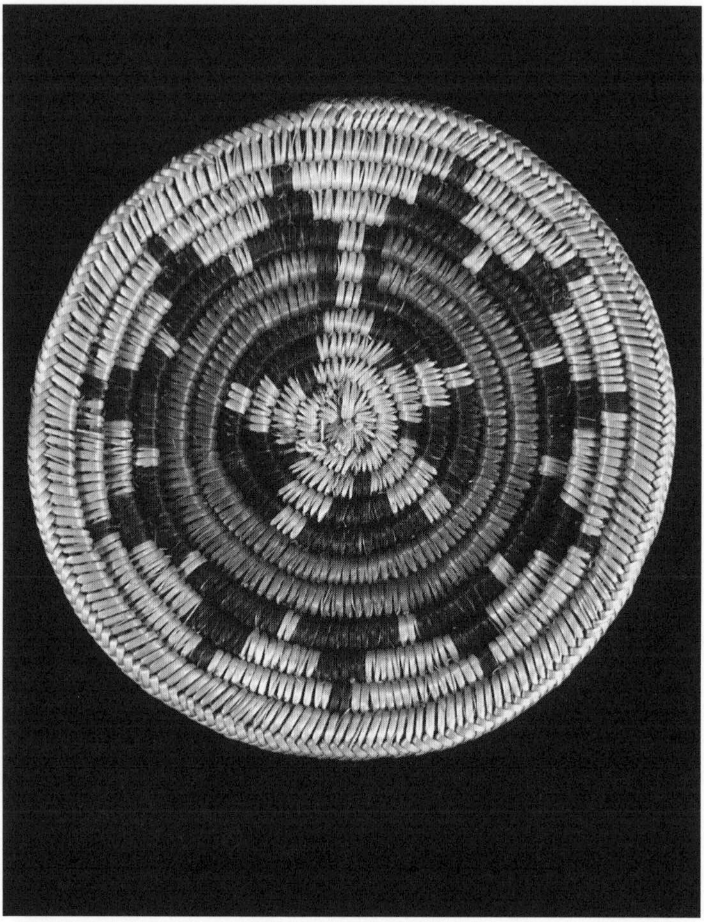

The designs in a Navajo wedding basket have a number of different interpretations, but one idea common to most is that of emerging through the center path of white. Just as the Navajo came through three or four previous worlds to this one, the concept of emergence is replicated in this basket.
(Photo by Stan Byrd)

CHAPTER EIGHT

Underworld and Emergence

Navajo and Anasazi relations started long before this world was created. In the four previous underworlds the Diné interacted with the Kiis'áanii, or Anasazi, on an intermittent but friendly basis. For example, the Hopi, Zuñi, and Taos peoples were created in the third world, where they worked with the Diné in harmony. As in the preceding worlds, supernatural means destroyed the third world, forcing the Diné and Kiis'áanii to move to the next sphere of habitation.[1] In the fourth world, the Kiis'áanii are depicted as "a race of strange men, who cut their hair square in front, who live in houses in the ground, and cultivate fields." Their friendship extended to treating the Diné kindly, providing food when necessary, and showing them how to construct rafts to prevent foot injuries when crossing a supernatural stream of red water. The Diné, in turn, held a council during which they decided to avoid any behavior offensive to their hosts and providers. The Kiis'áanii reciprocated by giving seeds of corn and pumpkin to plant.[2] When the Navajo women became domineering and a separation of the sexes occurred, the Navajo men invited the Kiis'áanii to accompany them across the river which served as the boundary line between the two groups. The puebloans went with the Navajo men but brought their own women with them. The two groups continued to travel together after the Navajo sexes reunited and moved to this, the fifth world. While resting during this journey, they "built a stone wall (which stands to this day), to lean against and to shelter them from the wind," though no specific archaeological site is identified.[3]

Although the Diné appear to differentiate between various tribes in the underworlds, all peoples, including the Diné, were not in the same form that they are today. Navajo mythology suggests that there was not only a marked distinction between the First People and the earth-surface people, or humans, but also between the Kiis'áanii and the Anasazi. One important difference was that people in their earlier existence held greater supernatural power. Whatever the variations, apparently what separated one group from another were cultural characteristics more than physical traits.

Differences then revolved around the question of degree. Since everything in this world had its prototype in previous worlds—including forms, powers, responsibilities, and physical qualities—the difference in a certain quality increases or decreases according to the state it is in. Some medicine men suggest that the line of demarcation between the First People and the Diné, or between the Kiis'áníi and the Anasazi, occurred after the formation of the clans which started on the Pacific Coast in the presence of Changing Woman. Others say that following the Emergence, Talking God and Calling God left the people, saying: "This is the last time that you have seen the diyin (holy beings) and you shall not see them again. . . . But when you hear the twitter and chatter of small birds, you will know that we are nearby."[4] It was at this point that the type and quality of supernatural power changed for the Navajo people.

Shortly after the Emergence, the Diné, realizing that they had failed to bring corn from the fourth world, demanded some from the Kiis'áanii. Following a brief dispute, they agreed to break an ear of corn in half and allow the Diné to choose between the two pieces. Coyote, the trickster, selected the tip of the corn and ran away, leaving the fuller stem behind, "and this is the reason the Pueblo Indians have today better crops than the Navahoes. But the Pueblos had become alarmed at the threats and angry language of their neighbors and moved away from them, and this is why the Navahoes and Pueblos now live apart from one another."[5] This incident helps explain the deterioration of relationships in this world, so that the Diné now view their companions of the past as estranged.

There followed a period of wandering by small groups of Navajos, during which their clan system originated. Leaving behind the more abstract worlds of mythology, the creation story is now tied to more concrete geographical areas and archaeological sites, many of which are associated with the clans. This is not to suggest that a smooth-flowing, historically provable narrative is evident, because many of the travels of the Diné vary from one version to another. What does emerge is a pattern of growing interaction that often results in conflict.

According to one account, the oldest Navajo clan is the Tséníjíkiní or Honeycombed Rock People.[6] Its descendants come from the first two human pairs who were "created by the gods from two ears of corn brought from the cliff houses of Tségihí, a canyon somewhere in the country north of the Rio San Juan, perhaps Mancos or McElmo."[7] Based on Navajo estimates, the couples' creation occurred "500 to 700 years ago [A.D. 1200–1400] or seven ages of old men." This is particularly interesting, not only because the chronology fits in with the tentative arrival of the Diné and the departure of the Anasazi, but also because this area was a favored home of the Navajo gods, or yé'ii, who lived in the ruins and cliff houses of the ancient ones.[8]

The importance of this clan is emphasized in another version of the creation story in which a group of Navajos wandered from Awatovi on Antelope Mesa and learned that to their north were holy people called Tsénííjíkiní, who lived in red rock houses. Others inhabited yellow rock houses, hence their name Tséńdziłtsooí. When these two clans disappear, so too will the Diné.[9] Although there is some confusion in this story because of the mixture of holy people with earth-surface people, the connection between the Anasazi and the Diné is indisputable.

There are many additional archaeological sites identified as the homes of the gods or as places of import in Navajo mythology. Sun Temple on Mesa Verde, White House Ruin (Kiníí' Na'ígai, or There Is a White Streak Across) in Canyon de Chelly, Chetro Ketl in Chaco Canyon, and Red Horizontal Rock (Tsénachii), somewhere north of the San Juan River, are all places where Navajo deities reside.[10] In a story connected with the Night Chant, a boy who was blind and another who was lame wandered to White House Ruin, where they met a yé'ii who was their father. He did not restore the boys to health, although it was within his power.[11] Another deity, Haasch'ee'ooghaan (Calling God), is noted for living in old cliff dwellings.[12]

An indication of this continuing Navajo interest in Anasazi ruins is given in a report by Dennis Fransted in which he surveyed dwellings outside of Chaco Canyon proper. As an archaeologist, Fransted identified forty-four sites, many of them minor, in a limited geographical region and then questioned Navajos living in the area. Approximately half of the locations had specific names and were associated with folklore and oral history.[13] Many of these sites and gods were woven throughout the songs and prayers that comprise the fabric of Navajo ceremonial practices.

The Kin Yaa'áanii, or Towering House clan, is another important group associated with the Anasazi. According to legend, a band of wandering Navajos settled among the people living in Chaco Canyon. There the Diné assumed the name denoting the architecture present and also received multicolored corn, which they planted. This was the first clan to do so. Eventually there were disagreements; the Diné killed some of the

Anasazi and so were forced to move on.[14] Washington Matthews, one of the earliest recorders of the Navajo creation myth, pointed out that the name High Pueblo House can be applied to hundreds of ruins on or near the reservation, but he believed the actual site was not in Chaco Canyon but was a six- or seven-story structure in Bernalillo County, New Mexico.[15] Regardless of the exact location, the general geographical area and the quality of the interaction indicate the importance of the Anasazi to the Diné during this period.

Other examples of the influence of the Anasazi come from the Dziłna'-oodiłłii clan, or Turning Mountain People, who joined another group of Diné and then removed objects from the cliff dwellings. There they procured pots and stone axes which allowed them to cook and make homes like the other people.[16] The Tábaahą́ clan built stone storehouses in cliffs in imitation of the Anasazi, while a raid against a pueblo called Kinłichíí' (Red House) near Ganado netted a captive woman who bore many children. The offspring started a clan of the same name. A similar incident at Jemez created the Mą'ii Deeshgiizhnii or Coyote Pass People clan, providing grounds for another claim by the Diné to Pueblo ancestry.[17]

Migrations continued as the Anasazi incurred supernatural displeasure that resulted in drought, warfare, and misfortune. The people of Chaco vacated the area shortly after the Diné arrived. Some moved to the Lukachukai Mountains, others to Mesa Verde, and others to Navajo Mountain. Oral tradition indicates that Keet Seel was built by the people from Navajo Mountain and Betatakin by those from Chaco, the settlers in each instance coming from two different groups who did not speak the same language.

Drought, wind, and hail continued to plague and weaken these people, who broke religious customs and married into their own families. Hunchbacked, deaf, and blind offspring resulted, while the surrounding canyons were bewitched and brought forth snakes. One informant stated that the Anasazi rock art found in this area is a depiction of the physical deformities these people engendered during this period of sexual license. Navajos wandered into the area and were shocked to see the Anasazi's plight and vowed that none of their people would marry into their own families. The Anasazi moved from Tségi to the top of Sleeping Ute Mountain, where they lived for some time, strengthened themselves, joined with others, and moved to Oraibi. The Táchii'nii clan (Red Running into the Water) "is the clan which joined us [Navajo] when the people came out of Tségi-Etso at the time of the great drought. They brought with them the

Night Chant. That is why it is their chant. It does not belong to the rest of us."[18]

Frank Mitchell, a Blessingway singer, suggests further indebtedness to the Anasazi for ritual knowledge. According to his account, the population in the pueblos expanded so quickly that they held councils in which they directed the people to move to holy places in the mountains, rocks, springs, and canyons and live there to enjoy a supernatural, everlasting life. Those who remained behind, however, continued to live a normal existence of birth, life, and death; but they could also communicate with those who departed. Eventually these people were destroyed by a tornado or big wind, but not before leaving behind a legacy. Mitchell states that "all these different chants like Male Shootingway, Female Shootingway, the Navajo Windway, and in fact all of them down to the small rituals, all these originated with these people and Holy Beings who used to live in the ruins."[19]

Some Navajos assume a more abstract approach to identifying the Anasazi. Matthews recorded a story suggesting that during the creative period, animals, birds, and snakes were just like humans and built homes near the Diné at Dibé Ntsaa, the most northern of the sacred mountains. They multiplied rapidly and those who had the ability to fly built dwellings in the cliffs.[20] One informant suggested that the Anasazi talked like cats, this observation based on the wind carrying the voices from their graves near an old site.[21] Others picture them as master rock climbers who must have had "sticky feet" in order to build homes and storage sites high in the cliffs. They also used shiny smooth stones to slide up and down the rock walls and canyons.[22] Still another insists that the lizards and horned toads are the descendants of the Anasazi, who were turned into this form because they displeased the holy beings. Proof of their previous human status is found in the five fingers on each appendage.[23]

Pueblo Bonito and Pueblo Alto in Chaco Canyon are often associated with stories about the Great Gambler. Navajos say that the Anasazi created watchtowers along the rim of the canyon, manned them with runners, and sent word to the gambler when a stranger approached.
(Photo by Joel Janetski)

CHAPTER NINE

Conflict and Dispersal

Many stories are site-specific and embellished with details, but all of them contain the general theme of conflict between the two groups. One account recorded in a number of different forms is that of the gambler known as One Who Wins You or He Who Wins Men at Play.[1] Briefly, the gambler was a divine person who descended among the people living in Chaco Canyon at Kinteel (Broad House). He enslaved the people by gambling and winning from them their rights to freedom, after which he demanded that they build the huge pueblo for his house. A group of Navajos wandered into this area to live and observed the gambler as he enslaved other people from Kin Dootł'izhí (Blue House). His pride even led him to refuse to give Jóhonaa'éí, the Sun Bearer, two shells he desired, and so the sun called the gods together and encouraged them to teach the haughty gambler a lesson.

The holy beings selected a young Navajo man, who had only been an observer, to be the instrument through whom the gambler could be defeated. They met with the Navajo man, instructed him, and sent him to participate in various games of chance. With the gods' help, the young man triumphed to such an extent that the people were freed and the gambler was shot into the sky as an arrow. There, he was helped by one of the gods, given new kinds of wealth such as sheep, mules, horses, swine, goats, and fowls, and returned to the earth as a leader of the Mexicans. Historically, these people confronted the Diné on the battlefield and used them as slaves in their homes, thus perpetuating the characteristics of the gambler.[2]

Another version that follows the general outline of this story suggests that the gambler was really an Anglo. Before he was shot into space, he warned the people, "In the future there will be round objects which the people will play games with to win. They will be a reminder of me."[3] The balls used in sports today that range from baseball and volleyball to basketball and golf are all part of the gambling wizard's heritage. He also had wind and lightning flashes as part of his power, and so promised that "when I return, everything that is round will roll beneath you with the wind. We will travel on the rolling rainbow arc." The Navajo relating this story then points out:

> Today, that is all very obvious. We travel on the highways with yellow and white stripes. A highway reminds us of the rainbow as it curves. The round objects under us are the wheels of whatever we travel in such as trucks, automobiles, trains, bicycles, and other things; and we travel with the wind. The lightning, I also know, has to do with electric current. People have lights in their homes and business places, along with all kinds of electrical devices. Taking these things together, One-Who-Wins-You must have been a white man.[4]

An additional effect of wind and round objects belonging to the gambler of Pueblo Bonito is tied to the destruction of the Anasazi. Round sandstone rocks that are fist-size or smaller and dark in color, and also round rocks that contain crystals and air pockets inside, known as concretions and geodes respectively, are called níyol bitsé, or "wind's rocks." When Navajo individuals pick up these stones, it is believed that a strong wind will start blowing. In the time of the Anasazi, a great wind whirled these stones about. The people hid from the harmful missiles and accompanying sand, shielding their faces with pottery or baskets from the blast only to die and be buried in the positions they are found in today.[5]

Navajo gamblers in the past performed a ceremony introduced by the great gambler. A man desiring supernatural power made a trail of goldenrod pollen from the hole of a green-collared lizard to his right hand, which contained more pollen. If the reptile emerged from its home and ate the pollen, the man was a full-fledged gambler and would always win; but if he flinched or forgot the accompanying songs, he would lose all that he had. The procedure was risky but one used with great effect by the legendary gambler.[6]

Members of the Salt clan ('Áshįįhí) recount how the Anasazi moved from the ruins at Aztec, New Mexico, to Pueblo Bonito because of drought. The gambler, then named Blue Feather because of a long blue feather he wore in his hair, came from far away in the south and joined them. He taught the men to chew a gum resin that served as a sedative, similar to alcohol or opium, and encouraged them to gamble until all was lost and the people near and far were enslaved. The Anasazi renamed him Ná'oolbįįh, The Winner. The plant identified as the one used by the gambler is named wire lettuce (*Stephanomeria pauciflora*), the root of which contains a narcotic gum said to "make one crazy."[7]

During his rule, he became despotic yet addicted to his own devices of gambling and gum chewing. He no longer took care of himself or his people, causing things to go from bad to worse. "The men gambled all the time. They did not take care of their corn fields nor did they perform any of their religious ceremonies." The gambler even broke a taboo and married a ceremonial, non-sunlight-struck maiden who served as a bride to the Sun. Droughts, early frosts, and poor crops followed until the people killed their leader, returned the woman to her ceremonial position, abandoned Chaco Canyon, resettled in Zuñi, and promised never to practice the ways of the gambler again.[8] Thus, whether the gambler was Mexican, Anglo, or Native American, he embodied undesirable qualities. These negative traits were then projected on alien cultures, the significance of which will be discussed later.

A story about Anasazi cruelty culminating in Navajo triumph in the Chaco area is found in "The Great Shell of Kintyel [Kinteel]," recorded by Matthews. The villages of Kinteel and Kin Dootł'izhí had two hunters who spotted an eagle's nest one day. Wishing to avoid any risks, they procured an old, beggarly Navajo man and bribed him with promises of food and wealth if he would climb into the nest and hand down the babies. The man got into the aerie, realized the evil designs of the hunters below, refused to do their bidding, and waited four days for the men and villagers to depart. He then visited the eagle people, with whom he had a series of adventures before returning to Chaco.

Upon reentering the villages, he set about ministering to the sick with the help of Navajos from Chaco and from the banks of the San Juan River. He told the people that if they provided him with strings of turquoise and shell beads to cover his legs, forearms, and neck, and gave him two large shells, one from each village, he would be able to heal them. During the last day of the ceremony, the gods protected the man by raising him into the sky and shielding him from the arrows shot by the angry Anasazi, who watched their wealth disappear with the old man.[9] Good again triumphed over evil in this story relating the basis for the Beadway ceremony.

An account concerning Aztec Ruins and the surrounding area tells of other forms of betting and competition. A race that combined running while kicking a round stone that whistled when it moved was one form of gambling. Batting balls with crooked sticks, pushing a circular disk on the ground, playing an activity similar to the Navajo stick game, and betting with a type of dice were other means used to waste time and become self-indulgent. The holy beings became unhappy with these activities, and so large pieces of ice rained down from the heavens, crushing people and pushing their homes into the ground, where they are found today. Some of the Anasazi were still sitting in them when they died and so were buried.

The ice eventually melted, but not without leaving dramatic proof of destruction—and a warning for today that Anglos are fast approaching the same point in their existence. "They [white men] are constantly playing ball. Over there the game was won like this, so many points, they won the game . . . . They have kept up without stopping, the Anglos have, and because of that they are killing each other."[10] After the gods destroyed the Anasazi, they became lonesome, and so they created more people, but people not "headed the wrong way."

The theme of slavery is again found in a story told by Manuelito, recorded by an itinerant trader, Don Maguire, in 1879. For many generations, the Anasazi were hard taskmasters over the Diné, forcing them to carry wood and corn on their backs for long distances and perform menial acts of service. Eventually, a large and handsome man came from the east, appearing to "rise out of where the sky and earth join together. He carried with him a long rod or staff. When he came amongst the Diné, he saw how they were being treated by the people who dwelt in the stone houses in the cliffs north of the San Juan River and he was very much displeased." He told them to stop this harsh treatment, but they replied they were "the greatest people in the world" and would do as they pleased. The stranger counseled the Diné that at the next new moon they should prepare a feast of turkeys, rabbits, corn, paper bread, and other delicacies and serve it at places on the south bank of the San Juan and Little Colorado rivers. They sent runners to the cliff dwellers, who were "great gluttons" and responded in large numbers. "They were first to cross from along the north bank of the San Juan River as the feast was spread along the south bank for a distance of about four miles, and as the horde of cliff dwellers came forward to take part in the feast, they rushed to cross the river." The stranger waited until they were in the middle of the river, then raised his arm to the level of his chest, twice waved his rod, and uttered some magic words. The Anasazi turned into fish instantly. He then faced westward and southwestward, pointed his rod in each direction, said the same magic words, and all the remaining cliff dwellers were struck with lockjaw and paralysis of the arms and legs. They died within four days.[11] By then, the Diné had eaten the feast they had prepared.

Manuelito did not divulge the name of the stranger because he was yet considered a friend. He did say, however, that this incident explains why traditional Navajos do not eat fish, the descendants of the cliff dwellers. Knowledge of this event extended beyond Manuelito, since in 1908 archaeologist Neil Judd reported being told the same story.[12]

Meanness and pride is again personified by the Anasazi living at Awatovi, Wide Ruins, Standing Willow, and south of the San Francisco Peaks. The people were "numerous as red ants all the way to Pueblo Bonito and the river." The Diné lived amongst them even though the Anasazi were proud and haughty because of their game animals, large farms, and fine houses. They became so controlling and abusive that they made the fatal mistake of imposing upon Monster Slayer, one of the Twins and supernatural hero of the Diné. He had a ceremony, held a council, and then joined his brother in a journey to Sun Bearer to enlist his aid in freeing the Diné.

Since Sun Bearer realized that this was the second time the Twins had made such a request (the first time to kill monsters inhabiting the earth), he refused to help unless he could have the "House Dwellers' souls." The Twins replied, "Don't say that, my Father. You ought to pity them and not ask their lives of us," to which he answered, "Do this favor now for me and I'll do anything you ask." The Twins reluctantly agreed, and on the appointed day Diné and Anasazi alike were slain when "winds came up and uprooted trees and stones, and clouds burst, and it rained and hailed for twelve full days. And the mountains were covered by water so that none could be seen. Ice floated everywhere and covered the whole surface," but then started to melt. At the end of twelve days, all had returned to normal and the holy beings repopulated the earth with those people who had been removed from destruction. To speak of this event during the summer is still a dangerous thing to do.[13]

While there are various explanations as to why and how the Anasazi died, the underlying theme is that they had an extensive knowledge that led to a haughty, uncontrolled pride and eventual destruction. The most common explanation tells of how creative they were in weaving baskets and fashioning pottery. Unfortunately, the designs placed on these objects were sacred and many started to copy them. They also invented tools that allowed them to plant larger fields and reap bigger harvests. The population increased in size but decreased in respect for the sacred. A type of design craze started where profane symbols were mixed with those of religious importance and placed on clothes, bowls, baskets, pots, blankets, rocks, and stone axes. The designs became more complicated and beautiful each day.

The old Anasazi realized what was happening, but the young people continued to use the symbols for their own personal pleasure—until the holy beings started to withhold the rain. Some of the people died of hunger and thirst while the religious leaders tried to placate the gods. This was to no avail. Huge tornados with swirling fireballs swept through the canyon and open areas killing the people, while a one-eyed monster and a one-horned monster killed those living on the mountains. All were destroyed.[14]

Mae Thompson, a Navajo woman, tells another version of how the Anasazi living in Canyon de Chelly painted abstract things, like wind and air, and caricatures of animals. The gods became angry, sent a whirlwind and fire, and destroyed life in the canyons and mesas. The black streaks of desert varnish that cover cliffs and rocks in the area are from the smoke and fire of this destruction.[15]

Variations of this story suggest different problems but a similar outcome. One account tells of how the designs on the pottery and baskets were reversed, spiraling in a counterclockwise direction. This suggests witchcraft and the abuse of designs given by the gods. The Anasazi also copied forms of lightning, rainbows, and the wind (nílch'i) on pottery, causing the gods to send the great wind which removed the air and killed the people as they slept or sat in their homes. The bodies were eventually covered with sand.[16]

Others suggest that the Anasazi copied water bowls, called tó 'asaa', used in ceremonies for producing rain. The holy beings became angry at the abuse of sacred powers and caused the people's destruction by drought and wind.[17] Many are found buried with a basket or bowl on or near their head because they were ashamed of their actions and so were hiding from the gods' anger.

Some Navajos also suggest that the Anasazi learned to travel with supernatural means but then abused the power. "They learned to fly . . . that is why their houses are in the cliffs . . . [but] the Holy Beings had their feelings hurt by it . . . [and] said it was not good and killed them off."[18] A more detailed account says the Anasazi were a highly gifted people who obtained their knowledge through prayer. They asked the gods to allow them to travel by lightning, which was granted. After a while, they started killing each other with it, which is why their dwelling places are often burned. "To use it [lightning] they had to go by high standards and when these were broken, they paid a price."[19] The gods removed the air and killed many as they knelt and begged for forgiveness. Archaeologists call this position a flexed burial. Another explanation of Anasazi destruction by fire came from a Navajo man who said it was caused by the same meteorite that made Meteor Crater near Winslow, Arizona.[20]

What comes forth from these examples is that the Anasazi experience is believed to closely parallel the thought and actions of the Anglos of today. Disrespect for the sacred, inventiveness, competition, and greed are qualities shunned in traditional Navajo society but accepted and in some cases encouraged in white America. A large majority of the people interviewed suggested that Anglos and nontraditional Navajos are walking the same path to destruction followed by their predecessors. One man made this comparison by saying:

> Just like now, the Anglos are designing many things. They are making big guns and poison gas. Whatever will harm humans, they are designing. What happened then [with the Anasazi] I am relating to what is happening now.... When they designed on their pottery, they reversed the drawings, yet people did not believe they were overly inventive. And that can lead to self-destruction. Now the Anglos are going up to the moon and space. Whatever obstacle is in their way, they will not allow it to stop them. Some are killed doing this and others return from their quest. Do these people believe in the Holy Beings or God? . . . The Anasazi built with ease [doo bil nahontl'ah da] houses in the cliffs. Their mind probably did all this and this was like a big competition between them. They started to fly and then got jealous of each other.[21]

White people also control the elements as did the Anasazi. Lightning in the form of electricity, rain obtained by cloud seeding, and travel through the air are all accomplished with ease. The Anasazi asked the sun for help to invent energy. They received permission and invented "all sorts of things similar to today's nuclear technology. When they used it, it worked so well that they went beyond their limits. The history of their culture was forgotten. The Sun was very upset."[22] They also no longer greeted each other by expressing clan relationships. "The people were crazy."[23] Thus, today the older people look at how younger Navajos act, observing that "children no longer know who their brothers and sisters are and therefore we are looking for another disaster."[24] The past serves as prologue for the future.

Pottery and other Anasazi artifacts have attracted white men to burial sites for well over a hundred years. To the Navajo, this interest in physical remains blinds the white man to the more important warning of destruction through lack of reverence. "The white men invent something new every day; the last thing they will invent is how to duplicate a human body with all its functions. That will end their existence." John Begay, Aneth.
(Photo courtesy of Field Museum, Negative No. 63228, Chicago)

CHAPTER TEN

Anasazi Lessons for the Future

Significant points can be gleaned from this survey of Navajo views concerning the Anasazi. One of the most obvious is that they play the part of a convincing antagonist who illustrates the undesirable qualities of greed, competition, pride, and the profane as opposed to the sacred. Just as tales about Coyote, the trickster figure, serve to teach correct behavior by illustrating the results of impropriety, so too the Anasazi move from an acceptable, sharing relationship to one of self-destruction. The Greeks called it *hubris,* an uncontrolled pride often maintained at the expense of others. For the Anasazi, the central theme of their tragedy revolves around "what could have been" as much as what actually occurred. To the Diné, they were a gifted people gone astray. The lessons from their existence are retold time and again in the stories and songs that teach of the ruins that dot the landscape. Indeed, the sites and artifacts serve as mnemonic devices that warn the knowledgeable that the sins of the past are still a threat to those living in the present.

On a more theoretical level, the Anasazi experience is rooted in the underlying tenets of Navajo perception. History, in a chronological sense, pulses with the flow of expansion and contraction, "from emergence followed by the return to the initial state."[1] The Anasazi fall into this pattern, illustrating a rise, flow, and decline in their civilization.

Their climax was achieved through supernatural help—as was their destruction, which was incurred by their profanation of the sacred. This concept is important because the Navajo universe centers on maintaining harmonious relationships between the earth-surface beings and the gods. The destruction of the four previous worlds hinged on improper behavior and the breaking of religious dictum. So too did it end for the Anasazi—and could end for the Diné—in this world.

> Through abuse of the things and relationships that were created, the Navajo can affect this cosmic tide, to the effect of their shortening the period

> to be lived in this world. So due to the pulsating movement that is occurring during and through this period of time, a certain circularity can be seen; the beginning and end of this world exhibit the same forms, after which a similar cycle . . . is to commence.[2]

Thus, the problems encountered by the Anasazi in the past mirror those faced by the Diné today. Improper use of electricity, fear of nuclear energy, broken familial ties, irreverence for the sacred, and competition and greed in the marketplace are all problems suggested by Navajos as having led to the destruction of their precursors. They can also lead to the demise of the Navajo people.

A final consideration is the controversial view that perhaps the Diné actually did interact with the Anasazi. If one assumes (and this is a big assumption) that this is a possibility, then perhaps these stories provide an untapped resource into understanding this ancient people. Some archaeologists suggest that the Anasazi were not as peaceful as initially portrayed and that perhaps the large sites like Mesa Verde, Pueblo Bonito, and other Chaco ruins were, in part, constructed or serviced by slave labor. Could the Diné have provided at least a part of this work force? The legends, at least, indicate a subservient and exploited relationship. At the same time, much puebloan mythology is concerned with the improper behavior of the people, the displeasure of the gods, and the subsequent abandonment of cliff-dweller sites. The people left with a desire to purify their lives and maintain humility. Some puebloans, speaking of the Anasazi ruins, claimed that their ancestors were "destroyed by a wind of fire."[3] This correlates closely with the Navajo view.

The issue of oral transmission of stories and lore is complex. The prevalent view is that much of Navajo religion was borrowed from puebloan peoples during historic times, but it is also interesting to note that as early as 1897 Washington Matthews suggested that the religion came from the Anasazi and not from historic tribes like the Hopi (Moki). He argues that there are obvious influences between the Navajo and Hopi peoples because of trade, marriage, and warfare,

> but throughout all of the Navaho legends so far collected, it is strongly indicated that the Navaho culture, where borrowed, came from cliff dwellers, from inhabitants of pueblos now deserted, and from wild tribes. The Mokis figure but little in the Navaho rite-myths. . . . In radical points of symbolism, such as sacred colors and the ceremonial circuit, the Navaho and Moki rites differ widely.[4]

While this is anything but conclusive evidence, it confirms the Navajo view, since a large majority of the interviews conducted for this chapter mentioned that the Hopi and the Anasazi were two distinct peoples.

Whatever may have been the actual linkages, the Diné believe that the Anasazi played an integral part in their early history. Moving through the underworlds to this world, they shared a common experience until the cliff dwellers strayed from the values of correct behavior and became domineering. Destruction ensued, leaving the Diné to ponder the vacant sites and scattered artifacts that dot the Anasazi lands. From these objects came lessons for proper behavior and a guide for living a harmonious daily life.

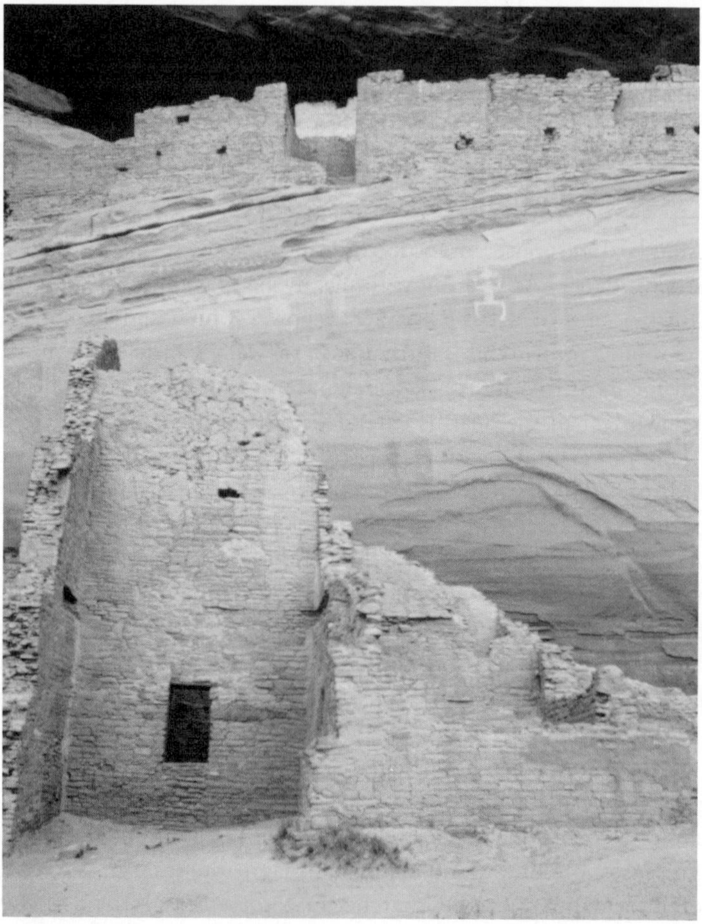

Anasazi sites, such as White House Ruin in Canyon de Chelly, hold special powers and dangers based on mythological events. One story tells of how some good Anasazi rid themselves of evil by inviting the bad Anasazi into kivas and then tossing a mixture of chili and ground bile made from the livers of eagles, hawks, and mountain sheep into the fire and sealing off the exit. The spirits of these evil ones may still haunt the ruins. (Photo by Joel Janetski)

Anasazi Sites

The standard response of most traditional Navajos to Anasazi ruins stresses avoidance. As with most things in the Navajo universe, there resides in the sites or artifacts a sacred power which should not be disturbed. Many informants say that just to walk in the ruins is reason enough for its spirits to attack a person and cause sickness. The Diné's well-known fear of the dead is extended to the Anasazi, who seem to be even more powerful in death because of the mythology surrounding their life and ruins. Gladys Reichard states that "a Navajo would risk freezing rather than seek shelter in such a house or lay a fire with wood from it."[1]

Even if a Navajo individual inadvertently stayed near a ruin, he or she might still be affected, because no one could be sure about the power of a place unless its history was known. Reichard tells of a Navajo woman who unwittingly camped on a trail that led to an ancient deer impound. She felt "weak all over" and became disoriented and confused, just as the deer had felt when driven into the yard. Thus, "a locality may be unsafe even for the uninformed because it is believed to be the dwelling place of the gods" or spirits from the past.[2]

People are warned from early childhood not to go into the ruins. Crippling diseases, blindness, and confusion plague the transgressor. A number of informants specified that because they were Navajo they were bothered by the spirits, or ch'į́įndii, whereas Anglos were not.[3] Fred Yazzie, a person raised in traditional beliefs, considered this to be true because the power is not real to others.

> If you are not scared of it, you can walk in there, . . . [but] when you are frightened of it, you will start seeing it. This is real to people who believe in it. If inside you believe there is nothing to fear, then you can go into these places and not be haunted by it.[4]

For those who do believe them to be sacred places, it becomes literally self-destructive to go into the ruins. The supernatural beings will start "gnawing" on a person, and thoughts will start to kill him. Thus, avoidance of the dead and their possessions help separate this supernatural power from the mundane, making the sites sacred and different from the everyday world.

Knowledge concerning ruins varies, as do the stories about them. What follows are some individual responses about the power and protection that emanates from them. One person suggested that the sites were important for their healing powers. This may be partly because of medicine bundles found at the sites (to be discussed later).[5] Some places are considered more powerful than others because of the remains of the Anasazi still buried there or lying on the surface. Another informant said that since smaller sites are often harder to find and less likely to be disturbed, they were usually more powerful than the larger, excavated ones. Also, during the spring and summer some ruins may have more potency than in the fall or winter, when powers and spirits are less active.[6]

The power at sites may also be concentrated to bring both good and evil. Practitioners performing any type of religious function there must first be ritually prepared, having participated in a number of Enemyway ceremonies before approaching the ruins. A purification ceremony is also performed after leaving the site. Medicine men, while there, have erected shrines in abandoned pueblo rooms and kivas. For example, one place of worship was located in a Lukachukai Basketmaker cist containing prayersticks made of Carrizo cane, lignite, turquoise, white shell, bird feathers, chert flakes, and rock nodules. Another shrine was located at a prehistoric pueblo on top of Crown Rock Mesa in the Steamboat Canyon region.[7] Because the rock is in the shape of a fish, the site and the mesa are used for rain-calling rites with prayers for good crops.

Perhaps because the Anasazi were so involved in agriculture, their spirits are appealed to in helping the Diné control insect pests. A number of anthropologists record the Navajo practice of taking destructive cutworms or grasshoppers to a pueblo and skewering the insects with a twig or mutilating them with an arrowhead, placing the remains on an ancient potsherd, and saying prayers to defeat the creature.[8] If the worm crawled off the sherd in the direction of the cornfield, the ceremony had failed. Reichard provides one of the most detailed descriptions of this practice when she writes:

> Four worms were collected, impaled, and turned inside out over twigs of slender sunflower. Then the cutworms were taken to a cliff-ruin kiva,

> where they were stuck into the earth flush with the ground, and covered with a potsherd. Four circles were drawn around the arrangement with an arrow point and it was left. The worms within the circles would have to disintegrate since they belong to the dead—they were inside out, they were buried in a place of the dead, and covered with an object that had belonged to the dead; the four circles left no way for tcindi [ch'į́įndii] to get out.[9]

As Reichard suggests, the ruins are viewed as the home of the Anasazi dead. They also served as a final resting place for the Diné. One burial site had been used earlier as a storage bin and only later became a tomb. Added to the circular Anasazi masonry was a roof of poles covered by a pile of stones. The body within the tomb was flexed and placed on its left side.[10]

Archaeologists such as Earl Morris, Alfred V. Kidder, and Ray Malcolm reported that Anasazi cists were highly desirable for tombs, having been used by the Diné not only in the past but also in "modern" times (1930s) as well.[11] Cosmos Mindeleff reported this same practice in 1897, stating that in the "older days" the Diné buried the remains of prominent leaders in the ruins of Canyon de Chelly. According to him,

> the number of burial cists in the canyon are remarkable. There are hundreds of them. Practically every ruin whose walls are still standing contains one or more, some have eight or ten. They are all of Navajo origins and in many of them, the remains of Navajo dead may still be seen. . . . The burial cists are usually built in a corner or against a cliff wall and occasionally stand out alone. The masonry is always rough, much inferior to the old walls against which it generally rests, and usually very flimsy. . . . The typical Navajo burial cist is of dome shape. The roof or upper portion is supported on sticks so arranged as to leave a small square opening in the top. Apparently at some stage in its existence this hole was closed and sealed, but examples were examined which were very old and one which was but twenty-four hours old, but in neither case was the opening closed. Doubtless the opening has some ceremonial significance; it is not of any actual use as it is too small to permit the passage of a human body.[12]

The sites become increasingly powerful with the addition of more dead—whether Navajo or Anasazi. The Diné believe that the dead must be treated with the same respect as the living and that failure to do so will lead to heart attacks or nightmares brought by the wind (nilch'i). These spirits move on the wind and do not die, but instead search out the transgressor.[13] Thus the burial site becomes a potent connecting link between

Betatakin Ruins. Snakes were frequent inhabitants in many of the old ruins such as Betatakin. The Navajo believe the Anasazi kept them as pets and so their offspring still reside there today. Perhaps part of this belief stems from the Hopi ceremony commonly known as the snake dance. *(Photo by Joel Janetski)*

the past and present, dead and living. To antagonize the spirits of the deceased is to tamper with one's health.

Yet there are also exceptions to the custom of avoiding anything that belonged to the Anasazi. In Canyon del Muerto in northern Arizona, certain Navajos used two Anasazi dwellings for storage. In the same area anthropologists discovered five Navajo burials in Antelope House Ruin, while eleven different rock-art sites mixed Navajo and Anasazi figures together. In some instances the later art was drawn directly over the earlier Anasazi work, a practice that many Navajos would consider taboo. Rock shelters with puebloan masonry were also used by Navajos for storage, while Anasazi cists served as animal pens, with hogans constructed nearby.[14]

Another ruin in the Shonto area provides much the same kind of data. A Navajo family moved into an Anasazi site, refurbished the stonework, and made a home similar to the Anasazi dwelling which was built seven centuries earlier. The Navajo dwelling is surrounded by prehistoric structures with the same type of masonry and boulder construction.[15] Here, too, the Diné have interspersed their own petroglyphs amidst those of the Anasazi. This occupation of Anasazi sites is not necessarily a new innovation, since some Navajos tell of living in them before and during the Long Walk to Bosque Redondo in 1863.[16]

These practices are in direct conflict with the teachings of proper conduct associated with ruins. For instance, one man was told by his parents that a large snake lived within the walls of Pueblo Bonito and that if he ever entered he would be destroyed. To talk about what Chaco Canyon looked like when this informant first saw it was too dangerous and could only be discussed in winter, or else he might be bitten by the snake or struck by lightning.[17] Thus, there are two lines of reasoning about the sites, one stressing they should be avoided unless a person is supernaturally protected, and the other suggesting that no special protection is necessary. The significance of this dichotomy is discussed later.

The contents of this medicine bundle reflect the importance of Paleoindian and Anasazi artifacts. Included in this collection are an Elko corner-notched point (5,000 B.C.–A.D 1,000), a Bajada point (5,000–3,000 B.C.), and a number of crescentic blades from the Great Basin. The gourd rattle has star patterns similar to Anasazi rattles. Additionally, there is a pitch-covered bullroarer with eyes and mouth of turquoise and a rawhide rattle with a buffalo tail.
(Photo by author)

CHAPTER TWELVE

Anasazi Artifacts

The ruins of the Anasazi also provide the Diné with many artifacts for both religious and secular purposes. For instance, they pick up potsherds found lying on the ground, crush them, and use them as temper in newly formed pottery to prevent too rapid a shrinking and cracking as the clay dries. Anthropologists first misconstrued one Navajo pottery-making site to be a place for Anasazi manufacturing because the Navajos had collected so much of the older pottery for their use. Others tell of how pottery is taken from ruins and used for drums in the Enemyway ceremony.[1]

Ceramic or rock pipes, popularly known among historic puebloan groups as cloud-blowers, are also taken from sites for ceremonial purposes. Described as being stemless or L-shaped with a bowl that has a hole in its bottom, the pipe is used when putting a Mountain Earth bundle together. It is smoked and the fumes breathed on the package after the contents have been wrapped, so that the burning tobacco will summon clouds, bring rain, and increase fertility associated with the bundle.[2]

Designs from Anasazi pottery and those painted or carved on cave walls are also familiar to the Diné. Byron Cummings, an early archaeologist in the Four Corners region, told of entering Bat Woman House in a branch of Tsegi Canyon in northern Arizona. On the wall was a large painted image of a bat woman interpreted by a medicine man to be associated with a story of Monster Slayer. After the hero killed the monster bird that lived on top of Shiprock, he needed help descending the rock cliff. He asked for aid from his grandmother, Bat Woman, who agreed to help if he would get into a basket she carried suspended on fine silken-like threads. She stipulated that he must keep his eyes closed while descending, which he did. According to the medicine man, a basket found in a nearby ruin is connected to this story and is the one in which Monster Slayer used to carry his arrows and sacred medicine. The ceremonial basket had two peculiar lobes at the bottom that represent the ears of Bat Woman. The design "represents in the bands of black and white the horizon lines of earth and light; the dark broad bands, the rain clouds; the dark triangles, the water jugs of the rain gods; and the white zigzag lines, the lightning."[3] Thus, Navajo mythology may be very specific in interpreting the significance of artifacts in the ruins.

The Diné identify another design as the Spider Woman pattern. Found on bowls and other ceramics, the design is a square with triangles at the corners. Spider Woman is a goddess associated with weaving and so it is not surprising to find this same pattern on baskets and blankets of the historic period as well as pottery of the prehistoric. Some sites also yield pieces of pottery with sawtooth edges called Spider Woman by the Diné.[4] Its exact use is unknown, but it appears to be associated with weaving.

Yet perhaps the most dramatic connection between Anasazi sites and pottery and Navajo medicine is linked to a specific type of bowl called a tó 'asaa' or water bowl. Beliefs concerning this artifact in both Pueblo and Navajo mythology concern the time of creation and clan migration. According to the Hopi, the gods gave each clan a small water jar to take on its wanderings through the desert. As the people settled in different areas, they buried their jars, from which water kept flowing. The holy man carrying this jar had to go without both salt and sleep for four days before he could remove the pottery and travel to the next site. Should the ceramic crack or break, a new jar was fired and replenished with ritually prepared sea water. The Hopi believe that

> when the jar is planted on a high mountain or in a sandy desert or near a village where there is not water, the materials in the jar will draw water from the distant ocean to supply you without end. The time will come when the villages you establish during your migrations will fall into ruins. Other people will wonder why they were built in such inhospitable regions where there is no water for miles around. They will not know about this magic water jar, because they will not know of the power and prayer behind it.[5]

Navajo mythology reinforces this belief. During the period of clan migrations, Anasazi people from the east visited the Diné, and the two groups settled down together. There they planted white, blue, yellow, and black pots at various locations, and these are where water and springs are found today. Also,

> at large ruins this water was put into large pots on the east side and this water sprang forth. This water may be collected at Navajo Mountain, San Francisco Peaks, Perrins Peak, Sisnajini, Mount Taylor, Taos at Streams-

> side-by-side, San Juan Mountains, and at the male and female mountains at Zuni salt lake.... In days to come, Earth-Surface People, when they come into being if they say this, "My Pueblo of old, its water I shall take out," and if one digs after it, at once water comes out.... Therefore, if you dig at such places and repeat the words, "I want to dig up Cliff Dweller water," the water will be found, they say.[6]

The Diné believe that at most sites the Anasazi took water from the sacred mountains; mixed it with pollen, clay, and other materials; then put it in a jar on the east side of the pueblo, where it can be found today. Described by contemporary Navajos as pottery painted with frogs, tadpoles, plants, or a design that has "openings," it still has power to bring moisture to the site or the region. The gods do not allow these bowls to be found unless the person is a medicine man who understands their importance and holiness.[7]

Cummings described what he believed to be a rain-producing pot in a cave in Monument Valley, Utah. On the slope in front of the cave were hundreds of bone, jet, slate, agate, turquoise, and shell beads; several pipes, arrowheads, and spear points; and bundles of sticks tied with yucca cord. Inside the cave was a black jar sixteen inches tall containing a string of fifty small wooden cylinders, thirty-six wooden pendants shaped like truncated cones, a string of forty half-gourd shells, a bundle of prayersticks and bone awls, and four carved wooden birds. Cummings thought this paraphernalia belonged to a rain-producing shrine. His interpretation, based on an analysis from an old Navajo medicine man, stated that

> the four birds of different sizes probably represent the messengers of the rain gods of the east, west, north, and south... while the wooden canopies... probably represented the canopy of heaven with the circle of the horizon, the homes of the rain gods of the east, west, north, and south, and the paths across the heavens which lead to the respective abodes of those deities.[8]

Thus, knowledge of the tó 'asaa' and the interpretation of rainmaking artifacts and symbols is an important aspect that connects the Anasazi to the Diné.

Anasazi tools are also used by the Navajo people. Arrowheads, which are often found around dwellings, figure heavily in ceremonial lore. When a point is found, the person inhales the air around it four times and asks for protection from the spirit accompanying it. Although some believe that arrowheads are made by horned toads that blow on a rock and chip it into a form with its breath, others believe that the Anasazi made these points and left them behind for the Diné's use. Just as Monster Slayer used arrowheads fastened to lightning to kill evil beings, so too did the Anasazi ward off fearful animals and enemies. The Diné also use the points for protection to shield them from supernatural harm, believing they come from the flint armor of Big Monster, which was shattered by the Twins' lightning bolts.

In healing ceremonies, the medicine man places the arrowheads pointing outward in a circle, touches them against the joints of the patient, puts them in a solution of herbs to drink, uses them to cut materials in the rite, ties them in the patient's hair (for four days), or stores them in a medicine pouch. Words such as "from behind this arrowhead the bad ailments will go," and "in the four directions black arrowhead will protect me" are chanted, so that the evil returns to its place of origin, afraid of the power contained in the points.[9] The analysis of one medicine bundle pinpointed the prehistoric site from which three arrowheads were taken and used for healing and protection.[10]

The Anasazi also left behind gourd and leather rattles that the Diné use in ceremonies. One type, in particular, is decorated with distinct star patterns—the Pleiades, the North Star, and the Big Dipper—and is used in the Enemyway ceremony. Other rattles made by the Anasazi and used by the Diné have deer hooves, strings, and special ornaments tied to them. Some of these are located in the Mesa Verde museum and have the same designs found on Navajo rattles, suggesting to some that these people were once related or had close interaction with the cliff dwellers.[11]

Of even greater consequence are the medicine bundles left behind by the Anasazi and subsequently adopted by the Diné. Cummings tells of excavating a small cave ruin in the Navajo Mountain area where he found an ancient pouch of deer hide with turquoise beads, pendants, and necklaces; two disks of polished jet; pieces of rock crystal; and some roots. A Navajo boy, present during this find, tried to take some of the items, but the archaeologists refused him access and so he brought an older man to the site. The Navajo man demanded, "This is my territory and these are my canyons and caves. Everything that is in them belongs to me and you must turn everything over to me and get out."[12] This is ironic since this man, Hosteen John, had guided the party to the cave in the first place. He felt strongly enough about obtaining the materials that he returned the next day with twenty warriors to back his demands. When the artifacts were still not handed over, he made amends and the issue was dropped.

This incident is particularly interesting because the pouch was of Anasazi origin, being found under "a couple of feet of debris." John did not mind the men digging there until it was unearthed, the contents reflecting similar items found in Navajo medicine bags. A number of informants heard this story and were asked to speculate on why John wanted the pouch and its contents. Responses varied but the general drift was that the items could be used in Navajo bundles for their supernatural powers. One man said that

> black jet and turquoise are part of the Navajo medicine bundle as is abalone. . . . He probably thought this is what we use to perform our ceremony and the medicine bundle was already blessed and holy. . . . He thought of using it for a good purpose and that it would be used by many generations to come. So we were the Anasazi he thought. . . . The medicine bundle once lived like us.[13]

Frank Mitchell, a very knowledgeable medicine man, believed that materials taken from ruins could be used with impunity as long as the practitioner showed proper ceremonial respect. He justified the use of arrowheads, shells, and other objects by pointing out that "those things come from our ancestors way back but they are not Navajo things."[14] At another time Mitchell stated that he had seen ceremonial objects that had been dug up and they were very similar to those used by the Diné today in the Shootingway ceremony. "The arrows, for instance, are only a little different. The feathers that are used in fletching these arrows are not split. . . . [There is also] the yucca leaf drumstick used for tapping the basket [used as a drum in Shootingway]."[15]

Not just the Diné believe in the powers of these pouches. In a recent interview, Earl Shumway, an inveterate pothunter, tells of digging in an Anasazi grave and stepping on a rattlesnake that bit him. He dreamed of "three long knives leaping out of the ground and stabbing him in the heart," which he associated with the body in the grave. He had uncovered an albino medicine man who had a "little pouch full of arrowheads and pouches of different smoke, herbs and pipes." Later, a dirt wall collapsed on Shumway and buried the site. He returned the next day only to break his ankle, and then a third time on crutches only to be driven away by "a nest of giant red ants [that] exploded upon him, stinging him from head to foot."[16] The supernatural powers of the dead man and his pouch were too much.

Spirits at sites are another phenomenon suggested by some non-Navajos. Alfred Kidder, an early Southwestern archaeologist, was eating lunch with a friend in a remote cave on Mesa Verde when

> suddenly from an unlocatable direction, though quite near at hand, a voice, loud and harsh began haranguing us in an absolutely unknown tongue. It kept up for nearly half a minute.... The voice seemed very angry about something, and carried such an air of righteous indignation that my first instinct was to apologize for whatever it was that was displeasing him.[17]

Kidder and his friend went to the mouth of the cave, but saw nothing. For a similar reason, Navajos refused to live around the ruins of Chaco—because "there were too many dead people there."[18]

Yet the spirits dwelling in these sites can also be beneficent. Healing powers of these holy beings are invoked through the practice of placing carved, wooden figurines in ruins.[19] A substantial body of literature already exists to explain this phenomenon, and so only a cursory description is provided here as one more example of the importance of supernatural aid located in Anasazi sites. Archaeologists and other investigators have found over eighty wooden figurines at different prehistoric locations, primarily in the eastern and central parts of the Navajo reservation.[20] These objects were placed there as part of a healing ceremony to return a sick person to a state of balance and harmony in nature. The illness may be caused "when the death of a snake, duck, chicken, bear, dog, pig, or a child has been witnessed by a pregnant woman or by her husband during her pregnancy, or have been at any time killed by them."[21] The sick person called in a medicine man, who carved an image of the offended creature or person and placed it in a ruin, accompanied with prayers and songs.

> The prayers... are recited in a foreign language but the fact that descendants of Hopi clans are usually called upon to make the dolls and images and recite the prayers would suggest that the language and the custom itself ... is of recent introduction and of Hopi origin.[22]

The actual curing ceremony ('anaalnééh) is relatively brief, less expensive, and unconnected to the longer ceremonial sings. The figurines may be either plain or painted and adorned. They are pressed against the soles, knees, chest, back, arms, and hands of the patient, then placed in a ruin "which is thought to be easily accessible to the supernatural."[23]

In one instance, a medicine man went to a ruin and asked the archaeologist doing the excavation to return a figurine. Another time a crew of Navajo workmen refused to be employed on a site because wooden figurines were located there. They believed that an object was at home on a site and belonged to the holy beings who reside there and restore the patient to health. To disturb it was taboo.

There are numerous stories that illustrate the anxiety felt by the Diné in the presence of Anasazi artifacts. One white man carried an Anasazi jaw with him as a security device; when he needed to leave his supplies unprotected, he merely placed the bone on top of the canvas covering the provisions and left. Although he found footprints in the vicinity, the Diné never touched the goods because of their proximity to the jaw.[24] Bones are accompanied by strong spirits and power. If a pregnant Navajo woman gets close to an Anasazi bone, the baby and mother may be affected. One child, whose mother was exposed to a bone wrapped in yucca fiber while being brought to an Enemyway ceremony, is said to have been born with deformed muscles, short torso, long arms, and mental retardation. Another person believes that cancer or "sores that do not heal" comes from contact with soil in which the Anasazi lie.[25]

Cummings tells of using wood from a ruin for his fires as he camped at an archaeological site. His Navajo guide was horrified to see the white men cooking over the blaze made from dead people's homes and assured them they would be affected "and maybe all the Indians get sick."[26] He thereafter dragged firewood across the sandy mesas and through the deep canyons in order to protect the archaeologists, as well as his family, from ill effects.

A trader at Wide Ruins had, near his post, a toolshed that exploded from a mixture of nitroglycerine and insecticides. The Diné refused to visit the store, believing that angry Anasazi ghosts had destroyed the building. Not until a medicine man performed a ceremony using his three medicine bundles containing petrified wood, feathers, and turquoise, and had chanted songs, planted prayersticks, and sprinkled corn pollen, did they consider the post safe to resume business.[27]

Richard Wetherill built this trading post near Pueblo Bonito in 1900 to capitalize on Navajo commerce. While trading there he was accused of doing illegal excavation of the ruins and using Navajo help to accomplish it. He was so proficient at obtaining artifacts that the Navajos named him "Anasazi."
(Photo courtesy National Park Service Archives, Santa Fe)

CHAPTER THIRTEEN

Traders and Archaeologists

Many whites have removed or otherwise disturbed Anasazi sites and artifacts through the years—and have had a negative influence on the reverence some Navajos have for those objects. There are numerous accounts indicating that both men and women operating trading posts encouraged the Diné to set aside their anxiety and guide people to the ruins, assist in the digging of artifacts, and locate objects on their own. Indeed, the traffic became so intense that in the *Report of the Commissioner of Indian Affairs* in 1905 the commissioner warned the traders that the artifacts from Anasazi sites were "not private property to be disposed of at will." The report continued:

> It is well known that for some years past, Indian traders have greatly encouraged the despoliation of ruins by purchasing from the Indians the relics secured by them from the ruined villages, cliff houses, and cemeteries.... Much of the sale of such articles is made through licensed Indian traders, to whom the Indians bring their "finds." It seems necessary, therefore, to curtail such traffic upon the reservation [Navajo, Southern Ute, and Zuñi] and you will please inform all the traders under your jurisdiction that thirty days after your notice to them, traffic in such articles will be considered contraband.... A failure to comply with these instructions will be considered sufficient ground for revocation of license.[1]

This decree apparently had little effect on most traders, since the traffic continued unabated.

The tenor of these transactions varied in scope, some of the traders being less zealous than others. A man in Shonto reported that after extended windstorms in the spring or intense cloudbursts in the summer Navajo shepherds brought into the nearby trading post pots, ladles, and bowls exposed by the storms. In exchange, the seller received five cents' worth of hard candy in a brown paper sack. Two Navajos took the trader to a site where they had been digging, only to find that the huge pot

One of the richest collections of Anasazi sites is in the Four Corners region. The Aneth Trading Post, built around 1885, was a frequent stopping point for archaeologists passing through the area. *(Photo courtesy Denver Public Library)*

located at the corner of the ruin had burst into three pieces, the pressure of the sand inside having shattered the jar outward.[2] Indiscriminate looting of sites not only removed valuable and perhaps sacred objects, but many pieces were probably ruined in the process. For example, Louisa Wetherill, wife of a trader in Oljato, received a basket that had been discovered twenty-five years previously by a man, who up until that time had not wanted to touch a thing that belonged to the Anasazi. With the trader present, his attitude changed.[3]

Another man sold an object that he had hitherto held to be sacred—a circular piece of sandstone one foot in diameter that was etched with an Anasazi petroglyph. He had used the rock for its healing power by rubbing sand off its edges and giving it to his patients. The cure was said to be effective against almost any disease. Still, he had been enticed to take advantage of its newfound value in the marketplace.[4]

Women were as active as men in collecting artifacts. A Navajo guide led Hilda Faunce, from her post at Covered Water, to a mound covered with sherds. Seizing a piece of broken bone, Faunce unearthed a skull and some vertebrae. A Navajo woman who was watching herded her children away, fearing that a "devil" might be present, while an old man warned Faunce to get the skull out of sight. She later found a bowl in the grave and proudly displayed it on her mantel.[5] While this was hardly in keeping with traditional Navajo values, Hilda saw nothing wrong with incorporating Anasazi materials as part of her decorating scheme. One can only imagine how the Diné viewed this use of dead people's property.

Navajos also entered the excavating business, some with excessive zeal. In 1906 one man took a plow and scraper and leveled a mound in order to get a few pieces of pottery to sell to the trader. He apparently destroyed much more than he saved.[6]

In addition to the purchase of artifacts, traders also encouraged Navajos to enter the ruins by enlisting them to work for archaeologists as laborers around the sites. The degree of willingness varied with each individual, but many sought employment simply because of economic pressures. How daring they became once hired was another story. Moving from the more timid to the more adventurous, one encounters a wide array of responses. For instance, Bill Lippincott, a trader at Wide Ruin, employed Navajos to help dig a ditch for a pipeline to his store. As the men labored with their shovels, they uncovered pottery, mortars, and beads. The Navajos thereupon refused to dig until the entire pipe system was rerouted, threatening to withdraw not only their immediate help but also future business at the post.[7] The trader realized that customer satisfaction in the supernatural realm was as important as in the merchandise that passed over the counter.

An archaeologist stabilizing part of Mummy Cave Ruin in Canyon del Muerto employed five Navajos to carry mud up the slope to the site, but they refused to enter in. On the other hand, Richard Wetherill hired some Navajos to dig in the Chaco ruins, which they did until they found an Anasazi corpse; then they quit. Eventually, though, others came looking for work, and the excavation reached a high of twenty Navajos employed in 1897. Fluctuation in the number of workers depended on economic conditions, the period around 1895 witnessing a serious national depression that affected the reservation as well as its surrounding area.

One of the problems Wetherill faced was that of his Navajo workers taking objects like arrowheads, figurines, and turquoise found during the excavating. Part of his solution lay in putting more than one workman in a room, hoping that the rivalry would cause one person to report the other's actions. This was not totally successful. One jet frog figurine with jeweled eyes appeared at a trading post in Farmington; Wetherill spent fifty dollars to get it back. He also sent his wife amongst the Diné to purchase any arrowheads they happened to have.[8]

The danger of coming into contact with the dead was believed to be lessened by ceremonial control of the evil. Earl Morris, while digging in Canyon del Muerto, hired a Navajo, old Seechi (or Shicheii), to dig. He agreed, since no corpse had as yet been uncovered. He refused the proffered face mask to protect his lungs from the dust, and soon he became sick. He sought out a medicine man, who prescribed a sweat bath, sang songs, gave powder to sprinkle on the Anasazi bodies, and suggested he wear the mask. The cure took effect and Seechi continued his work unmolested.[9]

Not all illness responded as rapidly. A group of archaeologists hired Frank Mitchell, a Blessingway singer, to work at Antelope House Ruin. Shortly after Mitchell dropped them off at the site, one of the men contacted him and asked him to do "just a small job." He found that the "job" was to help lift a mummy into his wagon and haul it to Chinle. Mitchell remembers seeing the dried skin and the dust-filled hair and smelling the strong stench of earth in which the body had lain. He explained his reactions by saying,

> When you are hired you are getting paid to do something you have been asked to do. You don't think about being afraid when you agree to work

> for someone like that regardless of what it is. You agreed to do it and you have to go through with it. . . . I did not handle that body at all. All I did was help lift it onto the stretcher. I did not refuse to go there with them because I was getting paid for it, but otherwise I probably would never have gone there because at the same time I was afraid of doing that.[10]

After he completed the task, Frank went home and scrubbed himself. But years later he became ill and consulted a medicine man. The diviner, using a hand-trembling technique, determined that Frank's contact with the mummy had caused his sickness. The medicine man prescribed an Enemyway ceremony and Frank was cured.

The intentional defacement of this Anasazi petroglyph suggests ritual killing of the figure. Located on the Navajo side of the San Juan River and across from a ruin, this form was probably associated with witchcraft and the dispelling of evil. Interestingly, many of the marks on the figure are in the same places as yucca fiber worn by participants in the Evilway Ceremony. The fibers, which represent pain and evil, are cut off at the conclusion of the rite.
(Photo by Winston Hurst)

CHAPTER FOURTEEN

Witchcraft and Protection

In addition to sickness, Navajos who go to Anasazi ruins may experience another negative effect—being accused of practicing witchcraft. The Diné believe that places where powers for good are concentrated may also have the capability of producing evil. Anasazi sites are a good example of how sacred powers that need to be shown deep respect may also be perverted and turned to evil.

One of the main elements necessary in the practice of witchcraft is a dead body.[1] For example, during the Enemyway ceremony an Anasazi bone or some hair is removed a few hundred yards away from the participants and a medicine man ritually shoots it. If this object is left alone for any time, witches may come by and steal it. They want the bone or hair for their own use as well as to prevent the good that comes from the ceremony.[2]

Other objects that can be turned to evil include wooden figurines and handprints pecked or painted on rock walls. Archaeologists have found statues in caves where witchcraft was reportedly practiced, while White House Ruin in Canyon de Chelly is noted for its association with the darker side of religion. Once an evil person has performed magic on an object, it may be taken to a site and placed there so it can take effect.[3]

Symbols painted on rock walls in or near the ruins may also have evil power. One woman, speaking about pictographs, explained:

> The Navajo has the same thing.... These drawings are close to where they conduct their witching. Those designs are not like people. They are not for the purpose of drawing but rather for witchcrafting.... Mesa Verde is probably made up of this and that is why there is little water there.[4]

Another person explained that the pictures were of animals and birds that the Anasazi killed and so the Diné had very strong feelings about them. Placing one's hands in the prints on the wall affected one's mind and feelings, causing "pain, headaches, jaw aches, arm aches, and gener-

Navajo avoidance of the dead is well known. Part of the explanation of this fear is that if a person died and was not buried properly, his spirit would roam the earth and find a home in a skeleton uncovered by erosion or lying close to the ground's surface. Handprints on walls, bones in ruins, and artifacts at sites belong to those who have gone before and who may be searching for someone to haunt. *(Photo by Winston Hurst)*

ally getting sick. It's going to be like a cloud over you. You won't realize it until you start having ceremonies and you walk out of the cloud."[5]

Respect is necessary to avoid offense, which may take either a spiritual or a physical form; to the Diné, there is often not a clear division. For instance, a painting left in a ruin was made for a reason, and the thought behind it continues to permeate its existence. Through the medium of the wind (niłch'i), which encompasses the living creatures of the world and acts as a supernatural messenger, the person who made the painting will be told that another is standing there copying his act. The ghost will haunt the living, causing its thoughts to enter the offender's mind. If the thoughts were evil, they become a part of that person's life.[6] One man described this phenomenon as "something that sticks to you like when a person has a cold and that person passes his cold on to you," while another said that when one goes to a "ghost place" his thinking will start "gnawing" him. A third person suggested that the dead spirit follows its pottery around when it is picked up by a living being, then bedevils him through nightmares during which kicking or movement is a sign that something is bothering the dreamer. Another said that what killed the Anasazi will be disturbed and return to destroy the living.[7]

In order to rid a person of these evil influences, one of two ceremonies may be used. Which one is used depends on how the Anasazi are viewed by the medicine man. Some Navajos claim that these puebloans are ancestors, and so the Hóchxǫ́ǫ́'jí (Evilway) is often used. It is effective against Navajo or ancestral ghosts that bother the living. The other ceremony—'Ana'í Ndáá', or Enemyway—is used against the spirits of Utes, Anglos, or other foreign enemies.[8] If the Anasazi are viewed in this latter category, then pieces of their bones or scalps are used to project harm upon them and thus rid the patient of the spirit causing the problem. In this ceremony, as previously mentioned, the medicine man, wearing only a breechcloth and carrying a gun, brings the object away from the group. At a certain place in the chant, after ashes have been sprinkled on the weapon, the bone is shot and left at that spot where the ghost was defeated.[9]

As with other aspects of Navajo and Anasazi interaction, the supernatural is closely entwined with the physical: symbols may express and even become the reality. A bone, some hair, or a manufactured item holds power that can be used for good or evil, depending on the intent of the practitioner. As in other elements of Navajo religion, there is a fine line between the physical and the supernatural, the living and the dead, harmony and destruction.

Hastiin Nalcoce Najaie and his son Chee. The Navajo teach their values through stories from father to son. The Anasazi represent an important understanding of not only the past but also the present and future. As Isabelle Lee, from Aneth, explains, "Once our people leave our culture and traditions, we will no longer have an identity. That is how the Anasazi destroyed themselves. They got carried away with their inventions, just like we are doing today."
(Photo courtesy Harold B. Lee Library)

CHAPTER FIFTEEN

Sacredness of the Anasazi

Throughout the preceding discussion, there have been two different lines of thought concerning Navajo use of Anasazi sites. The first is that the layman should avoid ruins, which are available primarily to medicine men who know the proper ceremonies and cleansing practices necessary to insure their own safety. Because the sites are powerful and have spirits and holy beings residing there, they are inaccessible to the uninitiated. The second line of reasoning is that the ruins are not necessarily different from any other location and so a person can freely enter the sites, use the materials there, and make whatever changes in structures or petroglyphs he deems desirable. No supernatural retribution will occur.

Little attempt is made here to establish changes over time or to differentiate between individual choice and tribal belief. A general pattern, however, suggests that the dichotomy in behavior can best be explained using ideas expressed by Mircea Eliade in *The Sacred and the Profane.*[1] Part of his thesis is that religious man separates the mundane world of daily life from the sacred, spiritual, religious aspects to make it special. "Interrupted space" exists where the sacred is found, and by differentiating the sacred from the profane the believer encompasses and identifies many values held dear. In other words, beliefs and values are highlighted by the object, location, or action considered sacred, embodying the most important elements of the religious experience.

Anasazi ruins and artifacts are two of many symbols important to the Diné. Their concern for the dead and those things associated with them is not only fear of punishment for profaning them but may also be understood in terms of deepest respect. There is, at times, little distance between the two. The sites and the objects convey the necessity of religious practice to solve the problems of daily life. As they show forth this power, they teach what is important.

For the Diné, sickness often involves the supernatural as much as it does the physical world. While both the Anglo and the Navajo cultures

Entering a site, such as this one in Grand Gulch, creates awe and a mystical association for those entering it for the first time. Mircea Eliade's explanation of "interrupted space" is beautifully illustrated for those who feel the "spirit" of a ruin. *(Photo by Winston Hurst)*

believe in cause-and-effect relationships, the cause for the Diné is most often associated with the supernatural, whereas the white man, generally, explains conditions in physical or psychological terms. Anasazi ruins make concrete the intangible and give a focus to the religious healing experience.

As a medicine man enters a site, he crosses a threshold into "interrupted space" where the safety of everyday life is exchanged for contact with the supernatural. In a sense, he follows a well-known pattern found in many myths—departure, initiation, and return. This same series of events is expressed in Navajo tales where a hero receives the knowledge and supernatural aid needed to survive a number of tests. By doing so, he gains access to an object or information necessary to bring back help to others. The hero then returns to the safety of the daily world with his new-gained power, object, or knowledge so that he can cure the sick, help the suffering, and maintain harmony with the forces of nature.

Perhaps the best example of this pattern is that of the Twins—Monster Slayer and Born for Water—who visit their father, Jóhonaa'éí, or Sun Bearer. The story starts with the boys leaving on a quest to find their father, who controls forces that can slay the monsters destroying the Diné. After a journey through obstacles that are overcome by supernatural aid, the Twins meet Jóhonaa'éí, pass another series of tests, receive lightning arrows, and return to their people to make the world safe. There are dozens of other myths that follow this same pattern of departure, initiation, and return, though the details differ.[2]

So it is with a medicine man. He ventures into a ruin, obtains an object or performs a ceremony, and does it in conjunction with the holy beings and spirits that reside there, although failure to follow properly prescribed ritual practices may endanger him once he has crossed the threshold. The uninitiated, on the other hand, are told to stay away because of the power.

A more difficult question is raised about those who have no fear of or respect for sites, even building their homes on or near them. Certainly part of the answer rests in the teachings that those people received in relation to the importance of the Anasazi. Because Navajo religious beliefs depend on the ceremonies and knowledge of the practitioners, there appears to be a variance in understanding in different geographical regions. Proof of this requires further research, but some informants suggest that people in certain areas of the reservation have a greater understanding and more respect than those in other places. A tribal-wide survey could be done to determine regional variations; but this becomes increasingly difficult, since the younger generation is not as aware of traditional practices.

Another source of variance in attitudes toward sites and artifacts is due to individual Navajos' contact with white traders, archaeologists, and Christian preachers who encourage change. Previous examples show that even those who believed in the spirits and powers of a site could be induced to overcome those fears for money. Perhaps those men who worked in the ruins placed sufficient faith in the cure that they would risk the danger, knowing that help was close at hand. Because Navajo religion teaches that a ceremony, if properly performed, will effect a cure, the healing aspect is not left to the whim of the gods but is seen as more of a contractual relationship. Correct performance equals healed patient.

The most important point to be made from this discussion is that the Anasazi sites were and are important to the Diné. They serve as repositories for objects and beliefs that are of imminent concern to traditional society. The tó 'asaa' for procuring ground water, the pipes to insure clouds and rain, the arrowheads for protection, the medicine bundles for ceremonial paraphernalia, and the figurines and bones and scalps of the dead for the performance of healing ceremonies suggest the major role these sites play in maintaining Navajo beliefs. As the ruins are mapped, excavated, and turned over to the public in the name of preservation, a destructive act occurs by unintentionally denying the medicine man religious access to sites and objects that had previously been available. This is not to suggest that ruins remain untouched, but only to point out the irony of preserving a "dead" culture while on the other hand inadvertently helping to deny a "living" one.

In summary, the Navajo use of Anasazi sites played an important part in religious beliefs. Although on the surface it appeared that they were simply and systematically being avoided, in reality the ruins had significant use by those who were ritually prepared to enter them. Extreme respect encouraged by the presence of supernatural powers helped separate these sites from everyday use and allowed them to be special places where aid could be obtained.

When the Anasazi left their homes and artifacts behind, they unwittingly bequeathed them to the Diné, as willing caretakers. Steeped in religious beliefs, the Diné utilized, yet unconsciously preserved, the Anasazi heritage. Now some of the responsibility has passed on to the white man, whose orientation is not toward the supernatural but the physical. Time will show whose approach was most successful in preserving the Anasazi legacy from the past.

Zuyah Chee. The beauty of Navajo culture is captured in both the features of this young girl and the teachings of the Diné. One man explained, "The sun claims us as his grandchildren and that is why we wear our moccasins, turquoise, and hair tied in a knot. He shines upon us all day long. Our Mother Earth stands adorned with all this same jewelry and somewhere between her and the sun, we people exist. The coils on the soles of our feet stand steadfast on the earth, and the coils of our scalp reach up to the heavens. So it is that we are recognized." John Begay, Aneth. (Photo courtesy Harold B. Lee Library)

Epilogue

"If I Were Awake, They Would Say I Am Their Child"

A Navajo student submitted an essay as a course project in a Native American literature class.* The student, in her mid-thirties, was raised with older Navajo practices and beliefs and speaks the language fluently. She belongs toward the end of the traditional scale on the imaginary cultural spectrum.

The student wrote about the inner conflict she felt because of her personal desire to fit in with her peers by wearing her hair down instead of in the traditional bun. Her mother constantly warned her that this was offensive to the holy beings and that Changing Woman had established the proper model to be followed. In one instance, before attending a traditional ceremony, the student, fearing that she might otherwise offend, acceded to her mother's wishes and wore her hair tied up. Later, after getting married, she changed her hairstyle and was soon visited by a man who told her, through stories, that to cut off her hair was to cut off the rain; at the same time, her grandmother lectured her that she had no self-respect if she allowed the holy beings to see her with short hair. She returned to wearing her hair in a bun but once again relented because other women had permanents and various hairstyles. She said, "I am ashamed to wear my hair in a knot. Each day I am forced by outside pressure to change myself to fit in a white man's world. I feel I do not know what my culture has to offer me."

Another time, she was chosen to carry the prayerstick in the Enemyway ceremony. Although this was a position of honor, she felt ashamed because she could not be with the other girls, some of whom were friends from school and were giggling at her. "I felt like running from the place with sacred ointments on me, but somehow I did not do that." She saw

* Permission to use this material was granted by the student, who wished to remain anonymous.

some men fighting at the ceremony during the time when they should have been "warring against the spirit of the enemy." She said, "They were blocking the supernaturals with their own blood. This is believed to be the cause of so many deaths in highway accidents, surgery, and fights. . . . If blood is spilled in the ceremony, it will affect the person who bled or his close relatives."

As she looked at the affluence of American culture, she compared its effects to the antics of Coyote, who could never have enough and so lived by deceit and overindulgence. She pointed out that rock music was too loud, that clothing went to extremes from the miniskirt to the maxidress, that garments were often designed to look torn and worn, and that people were never satisfied with what they had. Because of indoor plumbing, human beings now urinated in their homes—a practice introduced by Coyote in traditional culture to bewitch someone.

Even sleeping past sunrise was a problem. "At the crack of dawn, supernaturals come from the east to my home to bless it with favorable things or hardship and illness. . . . If I were awake, they would say I am their child. They bring blessings of hard goods, livestock, and knowledge." The student went on to say that alcohol abuse, unemployment, and the grinding poverty on the reservation are caused because "we are not willing to greet the supernaturals at dawn. I know I am trying to convert myself to another culture that looks easy, but it is not."

This woman's inner conflict to achieve equilibrium between two cultures is real and represents the problems of the more traditional part of the younger generation of Navajo people. The questions that she raises, the feelings that she has, will become increasingly intense as traditional values move further out of synchronization with the teachings accepted by younger Navajos. The older people just shake their heads and turn away, secure only in the knowledge that comprises their world.

Some people may feel this is a pessimistic view and hurriedly point to attempts to strengthen the religion, or they may use historical examples to show the adaptability of the Diné in the past. While these efforts are laudable, perhaps the teachings concerning the Anasazi provide the best mirror for self-examination. The fears of the elders, as reflected in these stories, tell of the loss of power, prayers, and protection. The myths and the supernatural beings are still there, but will they be recognized for the help and power that they have? Returning to the metaphor given earlier, the new generations of the Diné can "sleep" through the teachings of the elders or they can be like the student, who said, regarding the holy beings,

"If I were awake, they would say I am their child." The choice is an individual expression that every Navajo person will make. Whatever each decides, may it take him or her on a path of beauty over a landscape that has meaning and the power to teach and protect.

Notes

INTRODUCTION

1. Barboncito to William T. Sherman in council, May 28, 1868, as cited in J. Lee Correll, *Through White Men's Eyes,* vol. 6 (Window Rock, Ariz.: Navajo Heritage Center, 1979), 130–32.

2. Gladys A. Reichard, *Prayer: The Compulsive Word* (New York: J. J. Augustin, 1944), 16.

3. Joseph Campbell, *Myths to Live By* (New York: Bantam Press, 1984), 221–22.

4. Donald Worster, "Seeing beyond Culture," *The Journal of American History* 76 (March 1990): 1143.

5. Robert Rhodes, interview with author, College of Eastern Utah, San Juan Campus, November 20, 1989.

6. Mircea Eliade, *Cosmos and History: The Myth of the Eternal Return* (New York: Harper and Row, 1954), 92.

7. Campbell, 89–90.

PART ONE

Power, Prayers, and Protection: Navajo Sacred Geography of Southeastern Utah

1. W. L. Rusho, *Everett Ruess: A Vagabond for Beauty* (Salt Lake City: Gibbs M. Smith, 1983), 39.

2. See Richard F. Van Valkenburgh, *Diné Bikeyah* (Window Rock, Ariz.: Office of Navajo Service, U.S. Department of the Interior, 1941); Sam Bingham and Janet Bingham eds., *Between Sacred Mountains: Navajo Stories and Lessons from the Land* (Chinle, Ariz.: Rock Point Community School, 1982); Editha L. Watson, *Navajo Sacred Places* (Window Rock, Ariz.: Navajo Tribal Museum, 1964); Editha L.Watson, essay presented March 17, 1968, Doris Duke Oral History Project, no. 796, Special Collections, Marriott Library, University of Utah, Salt Lake City, Utah.

CHAPTER ONE: Mountains

1. Stephen Jett, "Preliminary Statement Respecting *The San Francisco Peaks as a Navajo Sacred Place,*" (n.p., n.d.), 2 (in possession of author).

2. Donald Sandner, *Navaho Symbols of Healing* (New York: Harcourt Brace Jovanovich, 1979), 196–202.

3. Sam Bingham and Janet Bingham, eds., *Between Sacred Mountains: Navajo Stories and Lessons from the Land* (Chinle, Ariz.: Rock Point Community School, 1982), 2.

4. James K. McNeley, *Holy Wind in Navajo Philosophy* (Tucson: University of Arizona Press, 1981), 19–22.

5. Charlotte J. Frisbie and David P. McAllester, eds., *Navajo Blessingway Singer: The Autobiography of Frank Mitchell, 1881–1967* (Tucson: University of Arizona Press, 1978), 210.

6. Martha Nez, interview with author and Baxter Benally, San Juan Historical Commission, Blanding, Utah [hereafter cited as SJHC], August 2, 1988; Mary Blueeyes, interview with author and Baxter Benally, SJHC, July 25, 1988.

7. Frisbie and McAllester, 202–3.

8. Charlie Blueeyes, interview with author and Baxter Benally, SJHC, August 28, 1988.

9. Robert W. Young and William Morgan, *Navajo Historical Selections* (Lawrence, Kans.: Bureau of Indian Affairs, 1941), 17.

10. Leland C. Wyman, *Blessingway* (Tucson: University of Arizona Press, 1970), 10–16; Chester D. Hubbard, *Hooghan Haz'ą́ągi Bó' Hoo' Aah: The Learning of That Which Pertains to the Home* (Tsaile, Ariz.: Navajo Community College Press, 1977), 13.

11. Stanley A. Fishler, "Symbolism of a Navaho 'Wedding' Basket," *The Masterkey* 28 (November-December 1954): 205–15.

12. Raymond F. Locke, *The Book of the Navajo* (Los Angeles: Mankind, 1976), 120–21; Linda Hadley, *Hózhǫ́ǫ́jí Hane' (Blessingway)* (Rough Rock, Ariz.: Rough Rock Demonstration School, 1986), 31.

13. Floyd Laughter, as cited by Karl W. Luckert, *Navajo Mountain and Rainbow Bridge Religion* (Flagstaff: Museum of Northern Arizona, 1977), 48–49.

14. Ibid., 31, 53.

15. Ibid., 49–50; Meta Atene, interview with Jean Atene, December 3, 1987 (in possession of author).

16. Claus Chee Sonny, as cited in Karl W. Luckert, *The Navajo Hunter Tradition* (Tucson: University of Arizona Press, 1975), 46.

17. Editha L. Watson, *Navajo Sacred Places* (Window Rock, Ariz.: Navajo Tribal Museum, 1964), 9; Charlie Blueeyes interview; Jett, 11–12.

18. Young and Morgan, 16; Billy Yellow, interview with author and Evelyn Yellow, SJHC, November 6, 1987.

19. Walter Dyk, ed., *A Navaho Autobiography* (New York: Viking Fund, 1947), 116–17.

20. Richard F. Van Valkenburgh, *Diné Bikeyah* (Window Rock, Ariz.: Office of Navajo Service, U.S. Department of the Interior, 1941), 27; Slim Benally, interview with author and Baxter Benally, SJHC, July 8, 1988; Hashk'aan Begay, interview with author and Baxter Benally, SJHC, July 1, 1988.

21. Van Valkenburgh, 167; Watson, *Navajo Sacred Places,* 9.

22. Florence Begay, interview with author and Nelson Begay, SJHC, April 29, 1988; Ira S. Freeman, *A History of Montezuma County* (Boulder, Colo.: Johnson, 1958), 166–67.

23. Slim Benally interview.

24. Ibid.; Mary Jim, interview with author and Baxter Benally, SJHC, June 7, 1988; Hashk'aan Begay interview; Tallis Holiday, interview with author and Jessie Holiday, SJHC, November 3, 1987; Curly Toaxedlini, as cited in Luckert, *Navajo Hunter Tradition,* 94.

25. Mary Blueeyes interview.

26. Gladys A. Reichard, *Navaho Religion: A Study of Symbolism* (Princeton: Princeton University Press, 1950), 464–66; Young and Morgan, 10, 13; Franciscan Fathers, *An Ethnologic Dictionary of the Navaho Language* (St. Michaels, Ariz.: St. Michaels Press, 1910), 35; Charlie Blueeyes interview.

CHAPTER TWO: Rock Formations

1. Billy Yellow, interview with author and Evelyn Yellow, San Juan Historical Commission, Blanding, Utah [hereafter cited as SJHC], November 6, 1987; Martha Nez, interview with author and Baxter Benally, SJHC, August 2, 1988; Floyd W. Laughter, as cited by Karl W. Luckert, *Navajo Mountain and Rainbow Bridge Religion* (Flagstaff: Museum of Northern Arizona, 1977), 52–53.

2. Slim Benally, interview with author and Baxter Benally, SJHC, July 8, 1988. This story was told by DJ, in an interview with the author. DJ, who is very knowledgeable about sacred geography, wished to remain anonymous.

3. Ibid.; Irene Price in conversation with Jim Kindred, 1978, as related to the author.

4. Martha Nez interview; Charlie Blueeyes, interview with author and Baxter

Benally, SJHC, August 28, 1988; Billy Yellow interview; Tallis Holiday, interview with author and Jessie Holiday, SJHC, November 3, 1987; Slim Benally interview.

5. Editha L. Watson, essay presented March 17, 1968, Doris Duke Oral History Project, no. 796, Special Collections, Marriott Library, University of Utah, Salt Lake City, Utah, 18 [hereafter cited as Duke, followed by the identifying number]; Richard F. Van Valkenburgh, *Diné Bikeyah* (Window Rock, Ariz.: Office of Navajo Service, U.S. Department of the Interior, 1941), 101; Billy Yellow interview with author; Tallis Holiday interview; Fred Yazzie, interview with author and Marilyn Holiday, SJHC, November 5, 1987; Billy Yellow, interview with Stephen Jett, SJHC, August 27, 1986.

6. Tallis Holiday interview; Watson, essay, 15.

7. Watson, essay, 15.

8. Billy Yellow interview with Jett.

9. Ibid.

10. Billy Yellow interview with author; Pearl Phillips, interview with Bertha Parrish, SJHC, June 17, 1987; Tallis Holiday interview.

11. Van Valkenburgh, 53; Martha Nez interview.

12. Martha Nez interview.

13. Mamie Howard, interview with author and Baxter Benally, SJHC, August 2, 1988; Mary Blueeyes, interview with author and Baxter Benally, SJHC, July 25, 1988. For additional information about prayersticks see Leland C. Wyman, *The Mountainway of the Navajo* (Tucson: University of Arizona Press, 1975), 20, 42, 46. See also Washington Matthews, *Navaho Legends* (New York: Houghton Mifflin, 1897), 213–14.

14. Luckert, 24.

15. Floyd Laughter, as cited by Luckert, 46; Luckert, 22; Buck Navajo, as cited in ibid., 92–93.

16. Mary Blueeyes interview.

17. Slim Benally interview; Mamie Howard interview; Charlie Blueeyes interview.

18. Florence Begay, interview with author and Nelson Begay, SJHC, April 29, 1988; Billy Yellow interview with author; Jim Dandy, interview with author, December 4, 1989; Billy Yellow interview with Jett; Charlotte J. Frisbie and David P. McAllester, eds., *Navajo Blessingway Singer—The Autobiography of Frank Mitchell, 1881–1967* (Tucson: University of Arizona Press, 1978), 314.

19. Franc Johnson Newcomb, *Hosteen Klah: Navaho Medicine Man and Sand Painter* (Norman: University of Oklahoma Press, 1964), 27–29; Watson essay, 21.

20. Florence Begay interview.

21. Matthews, 120.

22. Different versions of this story are found in Matthews, 119–22; Linda Hadley, *Hózhǫ́ǫ́jí Hane' (Blessingway)* (Rough Rock, Ariz.: Rough Rock Demonstration School, 1986), 29–30; Watson, essay, 14; Editha L. Watson, *Navajo Sacred Places* (Window Rock, Ariz.: Navajo Tribal Museum, 1964), 11; Tallis Holiday interview; Florence Begay interview.

23. Florence Begay interview; Van Valkenburgh, 144.

24. A number of versions with textual differences are found in Matthews, 96–103; Berard Haile, recorder, *Upward Moving and Emergence Way: The Gishin Biye' Version* (Lincoln: University of Nebraska Press, 1981), 207–16; Raymond F. Locke, *The Book of the Navajo* (Los Angeles: Mankind, 1976), 88–101; Charlie Blueeyes interview; Mary Blueeyes interview; Martha Nez interview; Slim Benally interview. For a chart comparing different versions of this story, see Leland C. Wyman, *The Red Antway of the Navajo* (Santa Fe: Museum of Navajo Ceremonial Art, 1973), 99–101.

25. Haile, 215; Wyman, *Red Antway,* 101; Charlie Blueeyes interview; Slim Benally interview.

26. Gladys A. Reichard, *Prayer: The Compulsive Word* (New York: J. J. Augustin, 1944), 415–16.

27. Wyman, *Red Antway,* 20; Wyman, *Mountainway,* 106–7.

28. Wyman, *Mountainway,* 19.

29. Florence Begay interview.

30. Slim Benally interview; Martha Nez interview.

31. Wyman, *Mountainway,* 117.

32. Florence Begay interview.

33. Tallis Holiday interview.

34. Pliny E. Goddard, *Navajo Texts* (New York: American Museum of Natural History, 1933), 177.

35. Mary Jim, interview with author and Baxter Benally, SJHC, June 7, 1988; Billy Yellow interview with author; Tallis Holiday interview; Slim Benally interview.

36. Wyman, *Mountainway,* 182–83; DJ interview.

37. The following oral histories discuss Kaa'yelli: Paul Goodman, Duke no. 689; Kit'siili, Duke no. 704; Eddie Nakai, Duke no. 723; Desbaa', Duke no. 703; Sally Draper, Duke no. 740; Ben Nakaidine'e, Duke no. 716; Navajo Oshley, Duke no. 735.

38. Navajo Oshley, Duke no. 735; Florence Begay interview; Martha Nez interview.

39. Wyman, *Mountainway,* 185, 189.

CHAPTER THREE: Earth and Sky

1. Gladys A. Reichard, *Navaho Religion: A Study of Symbolism* (Princeton: Princeton University Press, 1950), 470–75; Franciscan Fathers, *An Ethnologic Dictionary of the Navaho Language* (St. Michaels, Ariz.: St. Michaels Press, 1910), 35.

2. Washington Matthews, *Navaho Legends* (New York: Houghton Mifflin, 1897), 80; Franciscan Fathers, 35.

3. Ada Black, interview with Bertha Parrish, San Juan Historical Commission, Blanding, Utah [hereafter cited as SJHC], June 18, 1987, 1–2; Martha Nez, interview with author and Baxter Benally, SJHC, August 2, 1988; Franciscan Fathers, 41.

4. Frances Gillmor and Louisa Wade Wetherill, *Traders to the Navajos: The Story of the Wetherills of Kayenta* (Albuquerque: University of New Mexico Press, 1953), 222–24; Tallis Holiday, interview with author and Jessie Holiday, SJHC, November 3, 1987. For further explanation of the impact of the influenza epidemic see Robert S. McPherson, "The Influenza Epidemic of 1918: A Cultural Response," *Utah Historical Quarterly* 58 (Spring 1990): 183–200.

5. Editha L. Watson, essay presented March 17, 1968, Doris Duke Oral History Project, no. 796, Special Collections, Marriott Library, University of Utah, Salt Lake City, Utah, 8 [hereafter cited as Duke, followed by the indentifying number]; Linda Hadley, *Hózhǫǫjí Hane' (Blessingway)* (Rough Rock, Ariz.: Rough Rock Demonstration School, 1986), 20; Pliny E. Goddard, *Navajo Texts* (New York: American Museum of Natural History, 1933), 137.

6. Von Del Chamberlain, "Navajo Constellations in Literature, Art, Artifact, and a New Mexico Rock Art Site," *Archaeoastronomy* 6 (Winter 1983): 52–54.

7. Reichard, 406–13; Robert W. Young and William Morgan, *Navajo Historical Selections* (Lawrence, Kans.: Bureau of Indian Affairs, 1941), 14; Billy Yellow, interview with author and Evelyn Yellow, SJHC, November 6, 1987.

8. Billy Yellow, interview with Stephen Jett, SJHC, August 27, 1986.

9. Navajo Oshley, interview with Winston Hurst and Wes Oshley, SJHC, January 25, 1978; Charlie Blueeyes, interview with author and Baxter Benally, SJHC, August 28, 1988.

10. Martha Nez interview; Tallis Holiday interview; Slim Benally, interview with author and Baxter Benally, SJHC, July 8, 1988; Mary Blueeyes, interview with author and Baxter Benally, SJHC, July 25, 1988.

11. W. W. Hill, *The Agricultural and Hunting Methods of the Navaho Indians* (New Haven: Yale University Press, 1938), 71–72; Tallis Holiday interview.

12. Slim Benally interview; Matthews, 235; Karl W. Luckert, *Navajo Mountain and Rainbow Bridge Religion* (Flagstaff: Museum of Northern Arizona, 1977), 56.

13. Alyce Barrett, interview with author, SJHC, March 15, 1987.

14. Mary Blueeyes interview.

15. Andy Natonabah, comments at the Navajo Studies Conference, Tsaile, Arizona, November 3, 1988 (in possession of author).

16. Louisa Wade Wetherill, "The Woman Who Controls the Weather," *The Kiva* 12 (March 1947): 25–26.

17. Barre Toelken and Tacheeni Scott, "Poetic Retranslation and the 'Pretty Languages' of Yellowman," in *Traditional Literatures of the American Indian,* ed. Karl Kroeber (Lincoln: University of Nebraska Press, 1981): 72–73; see also Cecil C. Richardson, "Navajos Are Witty People," *Arizona Highways* 27 (August 1951):28.

18. Jim Dandy, interview with author, SJHC, December 4, 1989; Stephen Jett, "Preliminary Statement Respecting *The San Francisco Peaks as a Navajo Sacred Place*" (n.p., n.d.), 4 (in possession of author).

19. Hilda Wetherill, "The Trading Post—Letters from a Primitive Land," *The Atlantic Monthly* 142 (September 1928): 293.

20. Albert B. Reagan, "Sandstorm Protection of the Southwestern Indians," Reagan Papers, Special Collections, Harold B. Lee Library, Brigham Young University, Provo, Utah.

21. Reichard, 497; Matthews, 131; James K. McNeley, *Holy Wind in Navajo Philosophy* (Tucson: University of Arizona Press, 1981), 34–35; Ada Black interview.

22. Charlie Blueeyes interview; McNeley, 7–11; Ada Black interview.

23. Ernest L. Bulow, *Navajo Taboos* (Gallup, N.M.: Southwesterner Books, 1982), 11–12.

CHAPTER FOUR: Rivers and Streams

1. Frank Goldtooth, interview with Stephen Jett, n.p., n.d. (in possession of author).

2. Washington Matthews, *Navaho Legends* (New York: Houghton Mifflin, 1897), 211; Charlie Blueeyes, interview with author and Baxter Benally, San Juan Historical Commission, Blanding, Utah [hereafter cited as SJHC], August 28, 1988; Florence Begay, interview with author and Nelson Begay, SJHC, April 29, 1988; Editha L. Watson, essay presented March 17, 1968, Doris Duke Oral History Project, no. 796, Special Collections, Marriott Library, University of Utah, Salt Lake City, Utah, 22 ; Ada Black, interview with Bertha Parrish, SJHC, June 18, 1987; Fred Yazzie, interview with author and Marilyn Holiday, SJHC, November 5, 1987.

3. Matthews, 211; Charlie Blueeyes interview; Ernest Nelson, as cited in Karl W. Luckert, *Navajo Mountain and Rainbow Bridge Religion* (Flagstaff: Museum of Northern Arizona, 1977), 24, 113, 117; Long Salt, as cited in ibid., 40; ibid., 24.

4. U.S., Congress, General James Carleton to Headquarters, Department of New Mexico, March 21, 1865, *War of the Rebellion,* 55th Cong., 1st sess., ser. 1, vol. 48, pt. 1, 1232.

5. Charlie Blueeyes interview; Tallis Holiday, interview with author and Jessie Holiday, SJHC, November 3, 1987; Florence Begay interview; Andy Natonabah, comments at the Navajo Studies Conference, Tsaile, Ariz., November 3, 1988 (in possession of author).

6. Buck Navajo, as cited in Luckert, 103; W. W. Hill, *Navaho Warfare* (New Haven: Yale University Press, 1936), 12–13; W.W. Hill, *The Agricultural and Hunting Methods of the Navaho Indians* (New Haven: Yale University Press, 1938), 98–99.

7. Hill, *Agricultural and Hunting Methods,* 143; Fred Yazzie interview; Charlie Blueeyes interview; Jim Dandy, interview with author, SJHC, December 4, 1989.

8. See Leland C. Wyman, *The Mountainway of the Navajo* (Tucson: University of Arizona Press, 1975), 174–244.

9. Matthews, 134; Florence Begay interview; Nelson Begay, interview with author, SJHC, March 10, 1987.

CHAPTER FIVE: Plants

1. Sam Bingham and Janet Bingham eds., *Between Sacred Mountains: Navajo*

Stories and Lessons from the Land (Chinle, Ariz.: Rock Point Community School, 1982), 23–24.

2. Charlie Blueeyes, interview with author and Baxter Benally, San Juan Historical Commission, Blanding, Utah [hereafter cited as SJHC], August 28, 1988.

3. Washington Matthews, *Navaho Legends* (New York: Houghton Mifflin, 1897), 235; Tallis Holiday, interview with author and Jessie Holiday, SJHC, November 3, 1987; Fred Yazzie, interview with author and Marilyn Holiday, SJHC, November 5, 1987; Slim Benally, interview with author and Baxter Benally, SJHC, July 8, 1988; Charlie Blueeyes interview.

4. Cecilia Yazzie, essay dated December 1, 1987 (in possession of author).

5. W.W. Hill, *The Agricultural and Hunting Methods of the Navaho Indians* (New Haven: Yale University Press, 1938), 55–56, 60–61.

6. Bingham and Bingham, 24.

7. Mary Jelly, interview with Aubrey Williams and Maxwell Yazzie, January 21, 1961, Doris Duke Oral History Project, no. 772, Special Collections, Marriott Library, University of Utah, Salt Lake City, Utah, 16–18.

8. Mary Blueeyes, interview with author and Baxter Benally, SJHC, July 25, 1988; Gladys Yellowman, interview with author and Baxter Benally, SJHC, August 2, 1988.

9. Gladys Yellowman interview.

10. Cecilia Yazzie essay.

11. Mary Blueeyes interview; Gladys Yellowman interview. Unless specified otherwise, sources for information on plants are these two medicine women or Leland C. Wyman and Stuart K. Harris, *The Ethnobotany of the Kayenta Navaho* (Albuquerque: University of New Mexico Press, 1951).

12. Wyman and Harris.

13. Bingham and Bingham, 18.

CHAPTER SIX: Animals

1. Charlie Blueeyes, interview with author and Baxter Benally, San Juan Historical Commission, Blanding, Utah [hereafter cited as SJHC], August 28, 1988.

2. Ibid.; Jim Dandy, interview with author, SJHC, December 4, 1989.

3. Louisa Wade Wetherill, "Creation of Burro," *The Kiva* 12 (March 1947): 26–28; Charlie Blueeyes interview.

4. Charlie Blueeyes interview; Henry Jackson, interview with author, SJHC, February 3, 1989.

5. Christie Johnson, *Southwest Mammals: Navajo Beliefs and Legends* (Blanding, Utah: San Juan School District Media Center, n.d.), 7, 8, 9, 11, 17; Gladys Yellowman, interview with author and Baxter Benally, SJHC, August 2, 1988.

6. Charlie Blueeyes interview.

7. Ibid.; Gladys A. Reichard, *Prayer: The Compulsive Word* (New York: J. J. Augustin, 1944), 422–25.

8. Richard F. Van Valkenburgh, *Diné Bikeyah* (Window Rock, Ariz.: Office of Navajo Service, U.S. Department of the Interior, 1941), 10; Reichard, 384–85; Charlie Blueeyes interview; Donald Sandner, *Navaho Symbols of Healing* (New York: Harcourt Brace Jovanovich, 1979), 175–77; Johnson, 25.

9. W.W. Hill, *The Agricultural and Hunting Methods of the Navaho Indians* (New Haven: Yale University Press, 1938), 157; Franciscan Fathers, *An Ethnologic Dictionary of the Navaho Language* (St. Michaels, Ariz.: St. Michaels Press, 1910), 175; Charlie Blueeyes interview.

10. Navajo Oshley, interview with Winston Hurst and Wes Oshley, SJHC, January 25, 1978.

11. Sam Bingham and Janet Bingham, eds., *Between Sacred Mountains: Navajo Stories and Lessons from the Land* (Chinle, Ariz.: Rock Point Community School, 1982) 41–42; Karl W. Luckert, *The Navajo Hunter Tradition* (Tucson: University of Arizona Press, 1975, 100–102.

12. Luckert, 97; Hill, 102, 109, 110; Billy Yellow, interview with author and Evelyn Yellow, SJHC, November 6, 1987; Navajo Oshley interview. See also Francis H. Elmore, "The Deer and His Importance to the Navaho," *El Palacio* (November 1953): 371–84.

13. Jim Dandy interview.

14. Luckert, 97; Billy Yellow interview; S. P. Jones, interview with author and Sam Goodman, December 20, 1985; Mary Blueeyes, interview with author and Baxter Benally, SJHC, July 25, 1988; Reichard, 405.

CHAPTER SEVEN: Sacredness of the Physical World

1. *The American Heritage Dictionary,* 2d ed. (Boston: Houghton Mifflin, 1985): 1028.

2. Leslie Marmon Silko, *Ceremony* (New York: Signet, 1977), 2.

3. Mircea Eliade, *The Sacred and the Profane: The Nature of Religion* (New York: Harcourt, Brace and World, 1959), 11.

4. Betty Reid, "Shuttle Mission Faced 'Doom'; Council Recesses," *Navajo Times,* January 29, 1986.

PART TWO

Navajo Perception of the Anasazi: The Past as Prologue

1. For further discussion of this topic see David R. Wilcox and Bruce Masse, "The Protohistoric Period in the North American Southwest A.D. 1450–1700," Arizona State University Anthropological Papers, no. 24, 1981, 213–54; Robert W. Young, *Role of the Navajo in the Southwestern Drama* (Gallup, N.M.: Gallup Independent, 1968), 5–6; Stephen C. Jett and Virginia E. Spencer, *Navajo Architecture* (Tucson: University of Arizona Press, 1981); Frank W. Eddy, "Culture Ecology and the Prehistory of the Navajo Reservoir District," *Southwestern Lore* 38 (June 1972): 1–75; Florence H. Ellis, *An Anthropological Study of the Navajo Indian* (New York: Garland, 1974), 108–12.

2. David M. Brugge, "Navajo Prehistory and History to 1850," *Handbook of North American Indians,* no. 10 (Washington, D.C.: Smithsonian Institution, 1983), 490.

3. Robert W. Young and William Morgan, *The Navajo Language: A Grammar and Colloquial Dictionary* (Albuquerque: University of New Mexico Press, 1980), 114.

4. David M. Brugge to author, July 9, 1987.

CHAPTER EIGHT: Underworld and Emergence

1. Mary C. Wheelwright, *Navajo Creation Myth,* Navajo Religious ser. 1 (Santa Fe: Museum of Ceremonial Art, 1942), 45.

2. Washington Matthews, *Navaho Legends* (New York: Houghton Mifflin, 1897), 68–70.

3. Ibid., 77.

4. Berard Haile, recorder, *The Upward Moving and Emergence Way: The Gishin Biye' Version* (Lincoln: University of Nebraska Press, 1981), 171–72; Jim Dandy, interview with author, San Juan Historical Commission, Blanding, Utah [hereafter cited as SJHC], December 4, 1989.

5. Haile, 78.

6. In using Navajo place names, especially when associated with clan names, a great deal of confusion can arise. This is caused partly by the practice of calling a single place by a number of names, partly through the translation process, partly because of the time lag between when it was collected and the present (Washington Matthews, for instance, did much of his work in the late 1800s), and partly because until recently there was no standardized spelling of Navajo in wide use. Rather than rewriting or guessing at exactly what was intended, I have provided what the source has said without correction.

7. Frederick Webb Hodge, "The Early Navajo and Apache," *American Anthropologist* 8 (July 1895): 223.

8. Matthews, 238.

9. Haile, 171.

10. Editha L. Watson, *Navajo Sacred Places* (Window Rock, Ariz.: Navajo Tribal Museum, 1964), 19; Matthews, 251, 224, 36.

11. Watson, 20.

12. Matthews, 225.

13. Dennis Fransted, "An Introduction to the Navajo Oral History of Anasazi Sites in the San Juan Basin Area," National Park Service—Chaco Center, n.d. (c. 1980), in possession of author.

14. John Barbone, Blessingway singer, as cited in Sam Bingham and Janet Bingham, eds., *Between Sacred Mountains: Navajo Stories and Lessons from the Land* (Chinle, Ariz.: Rock Point Community School, 1982), 85–86.

15. Matthews, 242.

16. Paul G. Zolbrod, trans., *Diné Bahane': The Navajo Creation Story* (Albuquerque: University of New Mexico Press, 1984), 294–95.

17. Ibid., 308, 338.

18. Frances Gillmor and Louisa Wade Wetherill, *Traders to the Navajos: The Story of the Wetherills of Kayenta* (Albuquerque: University of New Mexico Press, 1953), 124–28; Karl W. Luckert, *Navajo Mountain and Rainbow Bridge Religion* (Flagstaff: Museum of Northern Arizona, 1977), 152–54; Harold Drake, interview with author, Navajo Mountain, August 24, 1989.

19. Charlotte J. Frisbie and David P. McAllester, eds., *Navajo Blessingway Singer: The Autobiography of Frank Mitchell, 1881–1967* (Tucson: University of Arizona Press, 1978), 178–79.

20. Matthews, 81.

21. Pearl Phillips, interview with Bertha Parrish, SJHC, June 17, 1987, 5–6.

22. Fred Yazzie, interview with author and Marilyn Holiday, SJHC, November 5, 1987.

23. Rose P. Begay, interview with Bertha Parrish, SJHC, June 17, 1987, 8–9.

CHAPTER NINE: Conflict and Dispersal

1. Washington Matthews, *Navaho Legends* (New York: Houghton Mifflin, 1897), 81–87; Sam Bingham and Janet Bingham, eds., *Between Sacred Mountains: Navajo Stories and Lessons from the Land* (Chinle, Ariz.: Rock Point Community School, 1982), 63–69; Tom Ration, as cited in *Stories of Traditional Navajo Life and Culture* (Tsaile, Ariz.: Navajo Community College, 1977), 316–18; Paul G. Zolbrod, trans., *Diné Bahane': The Navajo Creation Story* (Albuquerque: University of New Mexico Press, 1984), 99–112.

2. Matthews, 81–87.

3. Tom Ration, in *Stories of Traditional Navajo Life,* 318.

4. Ibid.

5. Bertha Parrish, interview with author, San Juan Historical Commission, Blanding, Utah [hereafter cited as SJHC], April 28, 1988.

6. Leland C. Wyman, "Notes on Obsolete Navaho Ceremonies," *Plateau* 23 (Summer 1951): 47; Lulu Wade Wetherill and Byron Cummings, "A Navaho Folk Tale of Pueblo Bonito," *Art and Archaeology* 14 (September 1922): 133.

7. Leland C. Wyman and Stuart K. Harris, *The Ethnobotany of the Kayenta Navaho* (Albuquerque: University of New Mexico Press, 1951), 50.

8. Ibid., 132–36.

9. Matthews, 195–208.

10. Frank Becenti, interview with Ernest and Nannette Bulow, July 28, 1971, Doris Duke Oral History Project, no. 1235, Special Collections, Marriott Library, University of Utah, Salt Lake City, Utah, 93–99.

11. "The Third Arizona Expedition," Don Maguire Papers, Utah State Historical Society, Salt Lake City, Utah, 166–69.

12. Neil Judd, *The Material Culture of Pueblo Bonito*, Smithsonian Miscellaneous Collections no. 124 (Washington, D.C.: Smithsonian Institution, 1954), 67.

13. Berard Haile, recorder, *The Upward Moving and Emergence Way: The Gishin Biye' Version* (Lincoln: University of Nebraska Press, 1981), 217–20.

14. Chris Atene, interview with Rose Atene, February 21, 1983 (in possession of author).

15. Irene Silentman, "Canyon de Chelly, A Navajo View," *Exploration* (1986): 52–53.

16. Fred Yazzie, interview with author and Marilyn Holiday, SJHC, November 5, 1987.

17. Pearl Phillips, interview with Bertha Parrish, SJHC, June 17, 1987, 6; Florence Begay, interview with author and Nelson Begay, SJHC, April 29, 1988.

18. Ada and Harvey Black, interview with Bertha Parrish, SJHC, June 18, 1987, 16.

19. Daniel Shirley, interview with author, SJHC, June 24, 1987, 2.

20. Ibid., p. 7; information provided by Stephen Jett in personal correspondence, December 12, 1989.

21. Fred Yazzie interview.

22. Baa' Yazzie, interview with Rose Atene, February 10, 1987 (in possession of author).

23. Lama Chee, interview with Rose Atene, February 19, 1987 (in possession of author).

24. S.P. Jones, interview with author and Sam Goodman, SJHC, December 20, 1985.

CHAPTER TEN: Anasazi Lessons for the Future

1. Rik Pinxten, Ingrid Van Dooren, and Frank Harvey, *The Anthropology of Space* (Philadelphia: University of Pennsylvania Press, 1983), 18.

2. Ibid., 19.

3. Henry Mason Baum, "Pueblo and Cliff Dwellers of the Southwest," *Records of the Past* 1 (December 1902): 360.

4. Washington Matthews, *Navaho Legends* (New York: Houghton Mifflin, 1897), 41.

CHAPTER ELEVEN: Anasazi Sites

1. Gladys A. Reichard, *Navaho Religion: A Study of Symbolism* (Princeton: Princeton University Press, 1950), 81–82.

2. Ibid.

3. Slim Benally, interview with author and Baxter Benally, San Juan Historical Commission, Blanding, Utah [hereafter cited as SJHC], July 8, 1988; Billy Yellow, interview with author and Evelyn Yellow, SJHC, November 6, 1987.

4. Fred Yazzie, interview with author and Marilyn Holiday, SJHC, November 5, 1987.

5. Rose P. Begay, interview with Bertha Parrish, SJHC, June 17, 1987, 8–9.

6. Slim Benally interview; Fred Yazzie interview.

7. Richard F. Van Valkenburgh and Scotty Begay, "Sacred Places and Shrines of the Navajo: The Sacred Mountains," *Museum Notes,* Museum of Northern Arizona, 11, no. 3 (September 1938): 29–33; also Stephen Jett, field notes, 1983 (in possession of author).

8. Jett, notes; Leland C. Wyman and Flora L. Bailey, "Native Navajo Methods for the Control of Insect Pests," *Plateau* 24 (January 1952): 97–103; W.W. Hill, *The Agricultural and Hunting Methods of the Navajo Indians* (New Haven: Yale University Press, 1938), 58–59.

9. Reichard, 536.

10. Leland C. Wyman and Charles Amsden, "A Patchwork Cloak," *The Masterkey* 8, no. 5 (September 1934): 133.

11. Ray L. Malcolm, "Archaeological Remains, Supposedly Navajo, from Chaco Canyon, New Mexico," *American Antiquity* 5 (July 1939): 4–20. See also Clara Lee Tanner and Charles R. Steen, "A Navajo Burial of about 1850," *Panhandle—Plains Historical Review* (Summer 1955): 110–18.

12. Cosmos Mindeleff, "The Cliff Ruins of Canyon De Chelly, Arizona," *Bureau of American Ethnology*, Sixteenth Annual Report, 1897, 168–70.

13. Fred Yazzie interview.

14. Patricia L. Fall, James A. McDonald, and Pamela C. Magers, *The Canyon Del Muerto Survey Project: Anasazi and Navajo Archeology in Northeastern Arizona* (Tucson: Western Archeological Center, National Park Service, 1981), 190, 191, 282, 310, 313, 319, 321.

15. William Y. Adams, "Navajo and Anglo Reconstruction of Prehistoric Sites in Southeastern Utah," abstract, *American Antiquity* 25 (October 1959): 271–72.

16. Fall, et al., 191; Cecil Parrish, interview with Aubrey Williams and Deswood Bradley, January 6, 1961, Doris Duke Oral History Project, no. 667, Special Collections, Marriott Library, University of Utah, Salt Lake City, Utah, 3.

17. Neil Judd, *The Material Culture of Pueblo Bonito,* Smithsonian Miscellaneous Collections no. 124 (Washington, D.C.: Smithsonian Institution, 1954), 345, 348.

CHAPTER TWELVE: Anasazi Artifacts

1. Lucy Harvey, interview with Aubrey Williams and Maxwell Yazzie, January 18, 1961, Doris Duke Oral History Project, no. 708, Special Collections, Marriott Library, University of Utah, Salt Lake City, 3; Susan Kent, "A Recent Navajo Pottery Manufacturing Site, Navajo Indian Irrigation Project, New Mexico," *The Kiva* 47 (Fall 1981): 189–96; Franciscan Fathers, *An Ethnologic Dictionary of the Navaho Language* (St. Michaels, Ariz.: St. Michaels Press, 1910), 288; Fred Yazzie, interview with author and Marilyn Holiday, San Juan Historical Commission, Blanding, Utah [hereafter cited as SJHC], November 5, 1987.

2. Franciscan Fathers, 295; Charlotte J. Frisbie and David P. McAllester, eds., *Navajo Blessingway Singer: The Autobiography of Frank Mitchell 1881–1967* (Tucson: University of Arizona Press, 1978), 205–6.

3. Byron Cummings, "Kivas of the San Juan Drainage," *American Anthropologist* 17 (April 1915): 278, 281–82; see also Byron Cummings, "The Ancient Inhabitants of the San Juan Valley," *Bulletin of the University of Utah,* 3, no. 3 (1910): 4.

4. J. A. Jeancon, "Excavations in the Chama Valley, New Mexico," *Bureau of American Ethnology Report,* no. 81 (Washington, D.C.: Government Printing Office, 1923), 51, 66.

5. Frank Waters and Oswald White Bear Fredericks, *The Book of the Hopi* (New York: Viking Press, 1963), 41.

6. Berard Haile, recorder, *The Upward Moving and Emergence Way: The Gishin Biye' Version* (Lincoln: University of Nebraska Press, 1981), 174.

7. Franciscan Fathers, 400–401; Slim Benally, interview with author and Baxter Benally, SJHC, July 8, 1988; Florence Begay, interview with author and Nelson Begay, SJHC, April 29, 1988.

8. Cummings, 280–81.

9. Fred Yazzie interview; Billy Yellow, interview with author and Evelyn Yellow, SJHC, November 6, 1987; Tallis Holiday, interview with author and Jessie Holiday, SJHC, November 3, 1987; S. P. Jones, interview with author and Sam Goodman, SJHC, December 20, 1985.

10. Albert E. Ward, "A Multicomponent Site with a Desert Culture Affinity near Window Rock, Arizona," *Plateau* 43 (Summer 1971): 120–21.

11. Fred Yazzie interview; Charlie Blueeyes, interview with author and Baxter Benally, SJHC, June 7, 1988; Florence Begay, interview with author and Nelson Begay, SJHC, April 29, 1988.

12. Byron Cummings, *Indians I Have Known* (Tucson: Arizona Silhouettes Press, 1952), 28–29; see also "Archaeological Expedition Suffers Greatly on the Desert-... Thrilling Tale Told of Trip across Monument Valley," *Salt Lake Tribune,* September 5, 1915.

13. Fred Yazzie interview; see also Slim Benally interview.

14. Frisbie and McAllester, 265.

15. Ibid., 151.

16. Carol Ann Bassett, "The Culture Thieves," *Science* (July/August 1986): 27.

17. Ann Axtell Morris, *Digging the Southwest* (Chicago: Cadmus Books, 1933), 193.

18. David M. Brugge, *A History of the Chaco Navajos* (Albuquerque: National Park Service, 1980), 154.

19. See Roger E. Kelly, R. W. Lang, and Harry Walters, *Navaho Figurines Called Dolls* (Santa Fe: Museum of Navaho Ceremonial Art, 1972); Albert E. Ward, "A Navajo Anthropomorphic Figurine," *Plateau* 42 (Summer 1970): 146–49; James N. Spain, "Navajo Culture and Anasazi Archaeology: A Case Study in Cultural Resource Management," *The Kiva* 47 (Summer 1982): 273–78.

20. Kelly, Lang, and Walters, 17.

21. Franciscan Fathers, 496–97.

22. Ibid.

23. Kelly, Lang, and Walters, 40–41.

24. T. Mitchell Prudden, *On the Great American Plateau* (New York: G. P. Putnam's Sons, 1906), 172–73.

25. Bertha Parrish, interview with author, College of Eastern Utah, San Juan Campus, October 14, 1988; see also Gladys A. Reichard, *Navaho Religion: A Study of Symbolism* (Princeton: Princeton University Press, 1950) 159; Rose P. Begay, interview with Bertha Parrish, SJHC, June 17, 1987.

26. Cummings, *Indians I Have Known,* 27.

27. Alberta Hannum, *Spin a Silver Dollar* (New York: Ballantine Books, 1944), 45–46.

CHAPTER THIRTEEN: Traders and Archaeologists

1. "Traffic in Relics from Indian Ruins," *Report of the Commissioner of Indian Affairs* (Washington, D.C.: Government Printing Office, 1905), 29–30.

2. Elizabeth Compton Hegemann, *Navajo Trading Days* (Albuquerque: University of New Mexico Press, 1963), 366–68.

3. Frances Gillmor and Louisa Wade Wetherill, *Traders to the Navajo: The Story of the Wetherills of Kayenta* (Albuquerque: University of New Mexico Press, 1953), 130.

4. David M. Brugge, *A History of the Chaco Navajos* (Alberquerque: National Park Service, 1980), 166.

5. Hilda Faunce, *Desert Wife* (Lincoln: University of Nebraska Press, 1928), 238–40.

6. T. Mitchell Prudden, *On the Great American Plateau* (New York: G. P. Punam's Sons, 1906), 172–74.

7. Alberta Hannum, *Spin a Silver Dollar* (New York: Ballantine Books, 1944), 24–26.

8. Ann Axtell Morris, *Digging the Southwest* (Chicago: Cadmus Books, 1933), 167; Frank McNitt, *Richard Wetherill: Anasazi* (Albuquerque: University of New Mexico Press, 1957), 143, 165–68; see also Brugge, 155, 159–60.

9. Morris, 191–92.

10. Charlotte J. Frisbie and David P. McAllester, eds., *Navajo Blessingway Singer: The Autobiography of Frank Mitchell, 1881–1967* (Tucson: University of Arizona Press, 1978), 149–50, 163.

CHAPTER FOURTEEN: Witchcraft and Protection

1. For a complete study of witchcraft and its association with the dead, see Clyde Kluckhohn, *Navaho Witchcraft* (Cambridge, Mass.: Harvard University Press, 1944).

2. Tallis Holiday, interview with author and Jessie Holiday, San Juan Historical Commission, Blanding, Utah [hereafter cited as SJHC], November 3, 1987; Daniel Shirley, interview with author, SJHC, June 24, 1987.

3. Roger E. Kelly, R. W. Lang, and Harry Walters, *Navaho Figurines Called Dolls* (Santa Fe: Museum of Navaho Ceremonial Art, 1972), 41–42.

4. Ibid., 41–43; Slim Benally, interview with author and Baxter Benally, SJHC,

July 8, 1988; Fred Yazzie, interview with author and Marilyn Holiday, SJHC, November 5, 1987; Florence Begay, interview with author and Nelson Begay, SJHC, April 29, 1988.

5. Daniel Shirley interview.

6. S.P. Jones, interview with author and Sam Goodman, SJHC, December 20, 1985; Berard Haile, *Soul Concepts of the Navajo* (St. Michaels, Ariz.: St. Michaels Press, 1975), 89; Fred Yazzie interview.

7. Tallis Holiday interview; Fred Yazzie interview; Billy Yellow, interview with author and Evelyn Yellow, SJHC, November 6, 1987; Charlotte J. Frisbie and David P. McAllester, eds., *Navajo Blessingway Singer: The Autobiography of Frank Mitchell, 1881–1967* (Tucson: University of Arizona Press, 1978), 294.

8. Billy Yellow interview.

9. Tallis Holiday interview; Berard Haile, recorder, *Upward Moving and Emergence Way: The Gishin Biye' Version* (Lincoln: University of Nebraska Press, 1981), 374.

CHAPTER FIFTEEN: Sacredness of the Anasazi

1. Mircea Eliade, *The Sacred and the Profane—The Nature of Religion* (New York: Harcourt, Brace and World, 1959).

2. For more examples, see Katherine Spencer, *Mythology and Values: An Analysis of Navaho Chantway Myths* (Philadelphia: American Folklore Society, 1957).

Acknowledgments

I wish to acknowledge the help of many people, without whom this study could not have been completed. Bertha Parrish and Baxter Benally served as expert interpreters and translators; they conscientiously clarified and developed the ideas of the elders. The Utah Humanities Council, the San Juan County Historical Commission, and the College of Eastern Utah—San Juan Campus provided funding and words of encouragement, while editor Howard A. Christy and the Charles Redd Center had the patience necessary to see the project through to completion. Thanks also go to my wife, Betsy, and to my children for their willingness to excuse Dad from some family activities in order to finish the manuscript. And finally, and most importantly, I express my appreciation to the Navajo people of southeastern Utah for sharing their ideas, expressing their confidence, and entrusting me with this information to pass down to future generations. It is to these people that I dedicate this book.